N

Culture and Crisis in Confinement

Culture and Crisis in Confinement

Robert Johnson
University of North Carolina
at Charlotte

Lexington Books
D.C. Heath and Company
Lexington, Massachusetts
Toronto

Library of Congress Cataloging in Publication Data

Johnson, Robert, 1948-
    Culture and crisis in confinement.

    Includes index.
    1. Prisoners—Suicidal behavior. 2. Prison psychology. I. Title.
HV6546.J63   616.8'5844   76-25322
ISBN 0-669-00860-5

Published simultaneously in Canada

Printed in the United States of America

International Standard Book Number: 0-669-00860-5

Library of Congress Catalog Card Number: 76-25322

To my wife, Deirdra, whose constant encouragement
was a source of strength that proved invaluable

Contents

viii

List of Tables

Foreword

I am tempted to use this space for an endorsement of Robert Johnson's book—a sense of decency, though, prevents me from doing this. As a former member of the research team to which Johnson also belonged, my eulogizing his work would probably be incestuous. It would also be a superfluous exercise, because the reader can find out for himself that he has a treat in store by simply skipping the next few pages.

Where a eulogy is improper, a brief exegesis may not be. The author's contribution in this work is in many ways unique, and some of the concepts underlying this book may not be self-evident to all readers. I hope I'll be forgiven for explicating what to others may seem very obvious.

Corrections and penology traditionally have been the monopoly of sociologists, and sometimes of experts in administration. Psychological or clinical concerns usually have been confined to the area of individual diagnosis—particularly to the ritualistic review of unrepresentative offenders.

Though it is obvious that much sociological discussion of prisons has taken the form of psychology in disguise, disciplinary boundaries have inhibited full development of such thinking. Prison researchers have generally not deployed clinical methodology in their inquiries. Where inmates have been interviewed, they have rarely been asked the sorts of questions that explored their feelings and perspectives in depth.

Mental health experts, on the other hand, have a disquieting propensity to attend to each human tree without regard to its contextual forest. Even where professional experience accumulates, the inmate or offender rarely gets the benefit of it. Though every clinician knows that social and environmental forces powerfully impinge on his institutionalized client—and that these forces are usually strong enough to undo "treatment" results—the "case-work" approach has survived in practice with all its pristine sterility. The approach survives because the clinician has neither the tools to highlight ecological and subcultural pressures, nor the means of influencing the environments of his clients.

If inmates are to be viewed and dealt with holistically, we must evolve interdisciplinary approaches—perspectives that do violence neither to the integrity of the inmate's feelings, nor to the social world that impinges on the convict, with the full gamut of threats, challenges and opportunities that it offers.

Robert Johnson's book is a holistic portrait in this sense of the term. It offers a "clinical" view, by examining the coping problems of individual inmates with sensitivity and empathy. It offers a "sociological" view, by relating cultural origins to modes of prison adjustment.

The book is "holistic" in that it *integrates* clinical portraits with cultural trends. This task is more easily described than it is addressed. In practice, it calls for considerable delicacy and much theoretical acumen. This is the case because integration is not juxtaposition or laundry listing. It is not the strained application of group stereotypes to unsuspecting individuals, nor the compartmentalization of the person into phenotypical and genotypical subportraits, which never meet.

Integration means to make sense of the impact of socialization as it emerges on the firing line of "here and now" challenges and pressure. It means to understand personal responses against the backdrop of group responses, which are filtered through the ineffable uniqueness of the individual.

Although the challenges of this enterprise are enormous, they are increased with the intrusion of moral or value issues. Johnson studies human adjustment to prison, which is an institution whose deployment has been deplored. Why should the failure to "adapt" to prison or the inability to cope with man-made stress be of concern to us? Is not the amelioration of inmate suffering a reactionary endeavor? Should we not abolish prisons, instead? The author's point would be that while prisons exist, and while people suffer in them, we have an obligation to ameliorate their suffering. Such an obligation does not rule out other efforts, such as those promoting decarceration, or diversion from prison.

There is also a value issue relating to Johnson's emphasis on the ethnicity of inmates, and on the impact of subcultural socialization on adjustment. "Here"—some will argue—"is the familiar white middle class gambit of seeing others (preferably minority groups) as mental health problems, and of denigrating the socialization process in nonwhite middle class homes."

To apply this argument to Johnson's book ignores (1) his evenhanded coverage of functional and dysfunctional subcultural themes, (2) his inclusion of middle class white inmates, and (3) the convergence of what we know (from other studies) with what Johnson finds. There is also Johnson's emphasis on the basic humanity of his subjects, and his skill in conveying their varying perspectives in their own words.

These (and other) facts will cut little ice with critics whose *real* point is that ethnicity must not be researched, and that all data on race lead to racism. The logical equation is spurious, but the fear is real. It is the sort of fear that can be dispelled only over time with acts that are based on knowledge, and that are spurred by a desire to preserve differences that have value to the individual, while supplementing deficits that impair the fulfillment of human goals. Such is the hope and the faith of this book.

Hans Toch

Preface

Our subject is the relationship between cultural or ethnic background and suicidal crises among men in confinement. Our focus is on psychological breakdowns experienced by Latin, black and white prisoners. We rely on clinical interviews to trace the concerns that spawn coping difficulties and crises for members of each group and we emphasize susceptibilities to prison pressure that are systematically related to preprison experience.

Introductory chapters are devoted to the literature on prison adjustment (Chapter 1) and the "typical" patterns of adjustment found among each cultural group (Chapter 2). Subsequent chapters contain descriptions of research methods (Chapter 3) and findings (Chapter 4). There is a separate discussion chapter for each ethnic group. Adjustment problems and crises among Latin prisoners are described in Chapter 5, and patterns of adjustment and breakdown among black and white inmates are considered in Chapters 6 and 7. The book concludes with a chapter devoted to the theoretical and practical implications of the research.

The few past studies that focus on self-destructive breakdowns in confinement do not tell us very much about inmates or about the impact of confinement. These studies are isolated from the major thrust of prison research, and are usually piecemeal statistical endeavors. Nevertheless, these studies report marked ethnic differences in rates of self-mutilation and attempted suicide: black males are consistently underrepresented, while Latin males are consistently overrepresented. White men tend to be either proportionately represented or overrepresented among victims of prison crises.

Differences in susceptibility to breakdowns in confinement may reflect differences in the degree of fit between free world experiences and the survival model called for in penal institutions. Most black inmates may be relatively resilient to the stresses of prisons because a manly, peer-centered, free world posture may be compatible with coping strategies that address the major problems of prison, which is a dangerous, male-centered world. Conversely, Latin inmates may be disproportionately susceptible to crisis in confinement because their family experience fosters an image of manliness (machismo), which may conflict with convict norms and which may require emotional supports that are unavailable in prison. Comparatively middle class or sheltered backgrounds shared by some white inmates may create susceptibility because such men may be insensitive to prison norms, may have difficulty maintaining their self-esteem in penal settings, or may lack reliable family supports.

Because men from different cultural groups approach confinement with different frames of reference, confinement is a qualitatively different experience for some inmates in these groups. When these inmates break down, their crises may reveal special susceptibilities created by specialized past experiences.

Their concerns are apt to go unrecognized, however. Cultural differences in adjustment tend to be overlooked in favor of more conventional prison perspectives, which discount stress and suffering and view coping failures as products of weakness, cowardice or insanity. Yet to respond effectively to men in crisis—to offer relevant helping services and to provide appropriate supports—we must attend to stress as it is experienced by the person. For many men, cultural factors play an important role in prison survival. This book may provide a basis for understanding and ameliorating their despair.

Acknowledgments

Support for this book was derived from a variety of sources. Funds provided by the National Institute of Mental Health (research grant 5 R01 MH 20696-02) and by the New York State Department of Education (Herbert H. Lehman Fellowship LF-14, 1971-75) were essential to this effort. Of equal significance to the work was the unfailing cooperation of New York State correctional officials and inmates. I must express deep appreciation to members of the criminal justice faculty at the State University of New York at Albany for critical reviews and modifications of the manuscript when it was at the dissertation stage, particularly Hans Toch, Marguerite Warren, Robert Hardt, Fritz Redl and Donald Newman. Hans Toch must receive special credit for this work. His continuing efforts to teach me to research, write and think effectively laid the groundwork for this book.

There are others who played important roles in this research and who deserve thanks. Notable among these are John J. Gibbs and James G. Fox, coresearchers and fellow graduate students at SUNYA, who conducted inmate interviews with great sensitivity and offered insights on the role of cultural background in prison adjustment. Methodological and analytic assistance provided by William Feyerherm, Chris Zimmerman and Paul Sutton proved critical at various junctures. Administration services rendered by Tony Pasciuto of the Criminal Justice Research Center are gratefully acknowledged. My thanks also to the editorial staff of Aldine Publishing Company for allowing me to use materials in Chapters 2, 5, and 6 that I had published in modified form in Hans Toch's *Men in Crisis* (1975). Finally, the technical quality of the manuscript is largely the product of painstaking efforts by Suzette Geary, Sarah Butler and Gerry Richardson in the typing and proofing of endless drafts and revisions.

Culture and Crisis in Confinement

1

Coping and Failing to Cope

Our concern is with cultural patterns of adjustment and breakdown in prisons and jails. The focus is on failures in coping, on sequences in which men meet obstacles they cannot overcome, and in which they experience personal crises that culminate in acts of self-multilation. The degree and type of impact confinement has on different groups of men is inferred from rates of self-mutilation and from classifications of motives for such self-destructive conduct. Patterns of susceptibility to prison pressure are traced (where plausible) to predispositions that stem from specialized cultural experiences. Culturally linked survival patterns are also related to a normative prison survival model and to less salient prison adjustment strategies and norms.

The use of the terms "ethnic" or "cultural group" in this book differs from the conceptions of such groups employed in traditional anthropological works. For some thoroughly isolated populations (such as Mennonites and tribal groups), a distinctive set of customs, values and mores may endure intact, and may form an interrelated whole. A more limited homogeneity characterizes the cultural experiences of Latin, black and white prisoners—one that includes personal attributes, values and norms shaped by larger American cultural experiences.

Modal experiences associated with ethnic background are described in Chapter 2. We first turn to an exploration of the literature on adjustment in penal settings, which views the psychological impact of incarceration upon the "average" male. His personal adjustment is seen as stemming from uniform deprivations assumed to characterize penal institutions, and leading to a set of prescriptions for survival embodied in convict norms of manliness and inviolability. Such literature does not address the question of the differential transfer value of "free world" experience in confinement. However, a picture of major problems and adaptations in prison provides a background against which the survival value of different cultural backgrounds may be assessed.

Psychological Survival in Prison

Imprisonment is a disheartening and threatening experience for most men. The man in prison finds his career disrupted, his relationships suspended, his aspirations and dreams gone sour. Few prisoners have experienced comparable stress in the free world, or have developed coping strategies or perspectives that shield them from prison problems. Although prisoners differ from each other, and may

1

feel the pressures of confinement somewhat differently, they concur on the extraordinarily stressful nature of life in maximum security penal institutions.[1]

Five "pains of imprisonment" have been enumerated by Gresham Sykes to describe stress in prison.[2] The confined man must contend with loss of liberty, deprivation of goods and services, deprivation of heterosexual relations, loss of autonomy, and loss of security. The real pressures of prison, however, go beyond the surface discomforts created by a harsh environment. Immobility, poverty, abstinence, compliance, uncertainity—each are aspects of the prison experience that seem designed to irritate and annoy. But the brunt of these pains of imprisonment lies in the fact that the prisoner has lost control of his world and is rendered powerless to alter his fate. The pressures of prison thus threaten to undermine the convict's image of himself as a self-sufficient, respectable adult male.[3]

Life lived solely in the company of men is likely to raise questions regarding one's status as a man. Such living conditions may, for example, arouse homosexual conflicts. The prisoner's male identity is apt to become distorted or blurred in this all-male world, where the moderating influence of women is conspicuously absent. Masculine concerns are further aggravated by the childlike subservience inherent in the convict's dependent role. Similarly, the prison ritual of "testing" men to identify potential victims keeps manly concerns in the forefront: The inmate is likely to feel that a personal confrontation is inevitable, and must therefore live with ever-present fear of failure and humiliation at the hands of his peers.[4]

Faced with substantial challenges and threats, inmates must evolve adjustment strategies that allow for personal survival. Their response is addressed to both the physical and psychological stresses of prison. The impersonal, spartan quality of prison life is to some extent relieved by patterns of interaction that place a premium on solidarity and sharing. Flagging self-esteem and doubts about personal adequacy are partially ameliorated by emphasis on criteria of manhood and worth that can be met by confined men.[5]

Convict behavior types or social roles[a] reflect attempts to address salient needs created by imprisonment; there are roles that relate to scarce commodities (merchants, punks, fags) and roles that represent collective ego ideals (real men, toughs). Taken together, these roles reflect an underlying need to evolve a dignified, manly image. The unacceptable or low-status roles are characterized by labels that imply femininity (fags, queens), abject weakness (punks, rats, center men), or adolescent impulsivity (gorillas, wolves, ball-busters, hipsters); higher status roles are described in terms of social cool and manipulativeness (mer-

[a]Argot roles are described by a variety of researchers. In addition to Sykes, this group includes: C. Schrag, "Leadership Among Prison Inmates," *American Sociological Review,* 19, (February 1954), pp. 37–42; H. Reimer, "Socialization in the Prison Community," *Proceedings of the American Prison Association,* 1937, pp. 151–155; R. Cloward, "Social Control in the Prison," *Social Science Research Council Pamphlet,* 1961, pp. 22–28; D. Clemer, *The Prison Community* (Boston: The Christopher Publishing House, 1940).

chants, politicians), or in terms of cold, calculating aggression (toughs, hard rocks). The model of decorum for the prison community is the "real man." Cool, aloof, in control of his emotions at all times, the epitome of the "hard, silent stoicism which finds its apotheosis in the legendary figure of the cowboy or the gangster."[6] However harsh or extreme this model may appear by free world standards, the ideal of composure in the face of emasculation opens the path to manhood and dignity to the convict.

The Manly Man

Accounts of life in such confined settings as Russian labor camps and French penal colonies share with modern characterizations of the prison experience a focus on the resilience and adaptability of their inhabitants. Dostoyevsky's protagonist in *The House of the Dead,* for example, comments on the uncanny ability of men to adjust to and survive the bestial conditions of nineteenth century Russian prison camps:

I don't understand now how I lived through ten years it it. I had three planks on the wooden platform; that was all I had to myself. On this wooden platform thirty men slept side by side in our room alone. In the winter we were locked up early; it was fully four hours before everyone was asleep. And before that—noise, uproar, laughter, swearing, the clank of chains, smoke and grime, shaven heads, branded faces, ragged cloths, everything defiled and degraded. What cannot man live through! Man is a creature that can get accustomed to anything and I think that is the best definition of him.[7]

A dramatic example of prison perspective is found in Solzhenitsyn's *The First Circle.* Gerasimovich, a man who had survived the worst the Russian prison system had to offer, advises an obviously distraught fellow prisoner that "there is probably only one path to invulnerability . . . to kill within oneself *all* attachments and to renounce *all* desires."[8]

Descriptions of the convict's version of decorum found in penal literature suggest that the attributes of manliness are universal norms regarding appropriate prison deportment.[9] Even the prisoner of war — faced with starvation, beatings, and the prospect of death in an alien setting — is required to maintain an impermeable "front of pride" before his captors.[10] While female inmates may legitimately advertise personal weakness and dependency in response to prison stress,[b] the male prisoner has a mandate to be proud, impervious, self-sufficient, and in control.

---

[b]Descriptions of adjustment norms in women's prisons can be found in: R. Giallombardo, *Society of Women* (New York: John Wiley and Sons, Inc., 1966); D. Ward and G. Kasselbaum, *Women's Prison* (Chicago: Aldine Publishing Company, 1965); and James Fox, "Women in Crisis," in H. Toch, *Men in Crisis: Human Breakdowns in Prison* (Chicago: Aldine Publishing Company, 1975), pp. 181–204.

The convict's image as a man who casually shrugs off the "slings and arrows of outrageous fortune" is promoted, in part, because it saves face for captor and captive alike. Recognition of human suffering would flood prisoners with unmanageable signs of weakness, and would present staff with interpersonal dilemmas. The pose of manliness is functional and departures from the model threaten to make routine interactions difficult. Implicit bargains are thus struck. Inmates support peer claims of strength and endurance, demanding reciprocity. Guards behave similarly. Unable to assist brittle men, they let the convict facade stand; and they may actively support convict norms by discounting genuine symptoms of stress.[11]

Such collusion between custodians and convicts is possible not only because guards wish to avoid unpleasant incidents or situations with which they are unprepared to cope, but because they, too, subscribe to the manly model.[12] Replated observations have been made about concentration camp guards, men for whom a popular pasttime involved hitting one another as hard as possible to test self-control and endurance.[13] Solzhenitzyn provides a telling characterization of the ideal Russian prison guard in *The First Circle:*

The officer on duty today was Senior Lieutenant Shusterman. He was tall, black-haired, and while not exactly morose, he never expressed any human feeling whatever—which was how guards were supposed to behave.[14]

A norm of manliness is not restricted to penal institutions. This pose may be particularly salient in penal settings, however, because alternative measures of personal worth are lacking. In the skewed world of confinement, the ideal becomes the baseline expectation. Except for behavior that flagrantly defies the assumption of personal dignity shared by prisoner and staff alike, and that may evoke open ridicule or victimization, departures from manliness are ignored, rationalized or suppressed.

Manliness in Context

While a norm of manliness and inviolability is described as universal in maximum-security prisons for men, the universality of this norm may be overstated. Research reveals modes of prison adjustment other than the "real" or "manly man" stance. Thus while many English convicts value traits of manliness (subsumed under the "Robin Hood" role), they also cite support from loved ones as a requirement of prison survival.[15] Concern with support of inmates has also been noted in peer-centered adolescent prisons.[16] Family support and assistance seem particularly critical for pretrial detainees. The stress of "rapid role transition" from citizen to inmate and the uncertainty regarding impending decisions by criminal justice personnel may make manliness a less salient coping option for jailed men.[17]

Factors linked to free-world experience, such as national origin, may also influence patterns of prison adjustment. Research conducted in Scandinavian prisons, for example, indicates that a norm of manliness, although prevalent, is not the primary coping strategy used by Scandinavian convicts. Scandinavians are prone to lack a "sense of honor" associated with criminal activities. They therefore develop an inmate social system which is less cohesive and antagonistic to staff than that of their American counterparts. Lacking a supportive peer subculture, they rely on a set of "defenses of the weak" to establish personal worth. They try to enhance their self-esteem at the expense of their keepers by confronting staff when official actions are in conflict with conventional Scandinavian norms. Rather than "taking it" when they feel they have been treated inequitably—as dictated by manliness norms—Scandinavian felons are likely to negotiate with prison staff, citing rules that have been been broken or ignored, or trying to hold staff accountable to general principles of equity in human relations.[18]

Attempts to "censor" staff as a means of neutralizing their power and building one's self-image may be more common in American prisons than has been suggested. Most inmates (regardless of national background) should experience confinement as somewhat dishonorable, and the number of inmates affiliated with cohesive, ego-supportive prison peer groups may have been exaggerated. Thus, many American inmates may on some occasions fall back on censoriousness as a means of self-defense.[19] Informal descriptions available in prison folklore and guard locker rooms regarding the extent of staff-inmate encounters featuring an equity theme in American prisons support this contention.

The nature and extent of prior criminal involvements may also shape the prison experience. Different criminal careers appear to produce different perceptions of the meaning of incarceration, which in turn are reflected in different adaptive strategies. Depending on the nature of their criminal involvements (for example, hard core junkie vs. professional thief), confined men can orient themselves primarily to the prison world or to the free world: Men can "jail," immerse themselves in prison life and strive for status and recognition in the prison community; they can "do time" and emerge from prison untouched by prison values, norms or mores; or they can "glean" by involving themselves in prison activities likely to have payoff in the real world.[20] Ethnicity and other important personal variables may prove relevant to preferred mode(s) of prison adjustment.

Manliness, then, is not the only, nor always the most salient, prison adjustment strategy. It is also an imperfect solution to prison problems. A stance of imperviousness may solve some prison problems; such as a pose may, for example, ward off potential inmate aggressors, or allow a prisoner to gracefully avoid unmanageable confrontations with staff.[21] The man who defines self-sufficiency as requiring reduced involvement with significant others in the free world—who feels he must keep his head "in prison" to survive—may find the pains of prison ameliorated because he can avoid disconcerting contacts with loved ones.[c] Manliness, however, may have double-edged impact, especially when the stance is overdone. A "supermanly" role may invite abuse from peers who wish to achieve "rep" in the prison community, or from staff who want to cement their authority.[22] Dissolving links with the free world may prove self-defeating, since the emotional support of intimates may help counter the loneliness and social isolation of prison.[d] In jail, where we note that significant others play an essential supportive role, a facade of independence is particularly brittle and susceptible to collapse.[23]

Another difficulty is that the "manly man" model solves problems by stipulating that problems do not exist, and thus makes no provision for feelings such situations may engender. Where a person suppresses strong feelings in order to remain alive (such as in prisoner of war or concentration camps), typical symptoms among survivors range from emotional flatness and apathy to hysterical loss of sight or hearing. There is also resentment and fear, marked irritability and suspiciousness, and the feeling that one is surrounded by threats.[e] Although the stress in a prisoner of war camp is more extreme than in a prison—and the "front of pride" that is employed entails much more than the calculated equanimity of the maximum security prisoner—these observations suggest that assuming a manly pose in confinement may carry a risk. Most prison inmates, it is true, appear able to conceal, deny, or suppress their needs without obvious side effects. But some break down as a result of denial of feelings.[24] The prevalence of chronic physical difficulties among prisoners may also relate to norms that dictate suppression of feelings.[25]

---

[c]Cohen and Taylor, for example, amass studies from a variety of sources that suggest at least some inmates find prison less stressful when they cut off contact with the free world. Their survey of "lifer's" in an English prison indicated that "there may also be some fatalistic relief in reducing the emotional reliance upon outsiders. It increases the individual's autonomy; it ensures that the absence of visitors or letters is not a recurrent worry, and that such absences do not provide opportunities for patronizing sympathy by officers." S. Cohen and L. Taylor, *Psychological Survival: The Experience of Long Term Imprisonment* (New York: Vintage Books, 1974). p. 67.

[d]T. Morris and P. Morris (*Pentonville: A Sociological Study of an English Prison* (London: Routledge and Kegan Paul, 1963)) found that some English prisoners can divorce themselves from the free world with impunity because they do not have any real commitments to life outside institutional walls: "prison walls for this minority are the comforting if unfeeling girdle of temporary security" (p. 165). Most convicts, however, attest to the critical role in prison adjustment played by significant others (p. 298).

[e]For prisoner of war camps, see: S. Wolf and H. Ripley, "Reactions among Allied Prisoners of War Subjected to Three Years of Imprisonment," *American Journal of Psychiatry*, 104 (1947); R. Spalding and C. Ford, "The Pueblo Incident: Psychological Reactions to the Stresses of Imprisonment and Repatriation," *American Journal of Psychiatry*, 129, No. 1 (1972), pp. 17–26. For concentration camps, see: H. Klein, "Holocaust Survivors in Kibbutsim: Readaption and Reintegration," *The Israeli Annals of Psychiatry and Related Disciplines*, 10, No. 1 (1972), pp. 78–91; W. Tuteur, "One Hundred Concentration Camp Survivors Twenty Years Later," *The Israeli Annals of Psychiatry and Related Disciplines*, 4, No. 1 (1966), pp. 78–91.

The ability to appear "cool" and in control, to maintain a stance of manliness, nevertheless remains a central feature of prison adjustment. Prisons confront a man with stress situations and the manner in which a man publicly reacts to stress may be more relevant to his fate in the prison community than how he really feels about stress. To "do time" or to "glean" in prison, an inmate must come to terms with the norm of manliness. Otherwise, he may find himself ostracized by his peers, and a likely target of pressure for sex or commissary items, or the subject of ridicule.[f] Similarly, censoriousness or reliance on family ties may appear "lame" by some prison standards, and invite staff harassment or peer abuse. Prison is not solely comprised of convict roles that pit "real men" against "sissies." But prison is a setting, as Genet has cryptically observed, in which "more than elsewhere one cannot afford to be casual."[26]

Stress and Breakdown in Confinement

To be sure, some men thrive in prison, and others seem able to make do with the resources available in penal settings. Such men have been the subjects of most prison research. A fundamental preoccupation of these studies has been with ostensibly successful adjustment strategies, even though various indexes of stress suggest that coping problems and crisis are comparatively common in confinement.[27] This bias may reflect the implicit assumption that survival and breakdown are separate and distinct phenomena characteristic of separate and distinct people. Whereas survivors respond effectively to environmental pressures and thus warrant study, men who survive only marginally represent idiosyncratic or atypical reactions to prison stress that are unimportant. Men who break down completely while confined are presumed mentally unstable or classed as "noncopers."[28] In either case, these men are viewed as an anomalous fringe group whose reactions are not relevant to the study of prison pressure.

Failure to cope need not reflect congenital or other defects, however, nor the mysterious absence of some trait or skill possessed by survivors. Prisons pose a wide range of challenges and threats, but provide few resources for psychological survival. It stands to reason that the preprison experiences of some men will make it difficult or impossible for them to cope with the special stresses of prison, or to satisfy basic needs in a cold, male-centered environment.

---

[f]A number of authors have suggested that expression of feelings, or behavior that connotes dependency or weakness, is often the first step toward stigmatization in prison. See particularly: W. Skelton et al., "Stress in Prison," in *A Handbook of Correctional Psychiatry, I,* (1968), pp. 1–11 (Document available from Bureau of Prisons); and E. Johnson, "Sociology of Confinement," *Journal of Criminal Law, Criminology and Police Science,* 51, No. 5 (1961), pp. 528–533.

8

Groups at Risk

Some social experiences may prove dysfunctional in penal settings. Adolescence, for example, may be associated with emotionality or dependency—attributes at odds with the manliness norm of prison; a rural upbringing or a history of victimization in city slums may make it difficult to endure confinement with equanimity because the urban "street corner" games played in prison may appear disproportionately novel or threatening. Vulnerable groups may be differentially exposed to prison pressure, or may variously lack the resources to combat normal prison stress.[29] The adolescent, naive or traumatized prisoners may be more likely to become victims of substantial peer abuse than their adult or urban counterparts. They may be unable to respond to routine prison threats. Middle class prisoners may find incarceration more stressful than lower or working class convicts because confinement may undermine middle class goals, remove ego supports, and penalize conventional middle class coping strategies. For Bettelheim, this sequence explains the plight of middle class persons in Nazi concentration camps:

They had little or no resources to fall back on when subject to the shock of imprisonment. Their self-esteem had rested on a status and respect that came with their positions, depended on their jobs, on being head of a family, or similar external factors. . . . Up to [imprisonment] they had never realized just how much extraneous and superficial props had served them in place of self-respect and inner strength. Then all of a sudden everything that made them feel good about themselves for so long was knocked out from under them. . . . [To cope] they tried to impress the guards with the important positions they had held or the contributions they had made to society. But every effort of this kind only provoked the guards to further abuse.[30]

Observations about the differential survival value of varying social experiences in prison are conjectural, however, because the issue has never been systematically explored.

Cultural Background and Prison Stress

Consistent with the tendency to view survival and breakdown as nonoverlapping phenomena, studies of self-destructive breakdowns in penal institutions do not attempt to relate their findings to more general issues of prison adjustment. They also fail to consider the implications of ethnic differences in self-destructive conduct.

Statistical studies show that relatively few black inmates injure or attempt to kill themselves in confinement; on the other hand, such self-destructive conduct is comparatively common among Latin prisoners.[g] The differences in breakdown rates is substantial enough to suggest that the free world experience of black and Latin inmates may be differentially relevant to the problems posed in penal institutions.

The behavior pattern of white inmates has been more variable than that of black or Latin men; presumably white inmates represent a more heterogeneous cultural group. Some studies report a disproportionate rate of self-destructive conduct among white prisoners, and others show proportionate rates of crisis.[h]

The explanations that have been advanced to account for ethnic differences in self-destructive breakdowns in confinement seem either too limited or too broad. For example, it has been suggested that Latin inmates are prone to injure themselves because of their unique sense of individual worth and singularity.[31] The black inmate, on the other hand, is less crisis prone because "he has never thought of himself as an individual; he has always been part of a group."[32] The only observation made with reference to the cultural determinants of self-destructive conduct among white inmates begs the issue by stating that their culture is "polyglot and mixed."[33]

Such observations have an all or none, stereotyped character. More plausible explanations are explored in Chapter 2, where we review a variety of historical and sociological studies of Latin and black cultures, and identify modal experi-

---

[g]Marked ethnic differences in rates of self-destructive conduct in both jails and prisons have been consistently reported. Almost invariably, blacks are underrepresented in the self-injury or suicide group. See T. Allen, "Patterns of Escape and Self-Destructive Behavior in a Correctional Institution," *Corrective Psychiatry and Journal of Social Therapy*, 15, No. 2 (1969), pp. 50–58; C. Claghorn and D. Beto, "Self-Mutilation in a Prison Mental Hospital," *Corrective Psychiatry and Journal of Social Therapy*, 13, No. 3 (1967), pp. 133–140; D. Beto and J. Claghorn, "Factors Associated with Self-Mutilation within the Texas Department of Correction," *American Journal of Corrections*, January-February 1968, pp. 25–27. B. Danto, "Suicide at Wayne County Jail: 1967–1970," in B. Danto (Ed.), *Jail House Blues: Studies of Suicidal Behavior in Jail and Prison* (Orchard Lake, Michigan: Epic, 1973), pp. 3–16; R. Espera, "Attempted and Committed Suicide in County Jails," in Danto, *Jail House Blues*, pp. 27–46; S. Heilig, "Suicide in Jails," in Danto, *Jail House Blues*, pp. 47–50; J. Faucett and E. Marrs, "Suicide at the County Jail," in Danto, *Jail House Blues*, pp. 83–106; W. Reiger, "Suicide Attempts in a Federal Prison," *Archives of General Psychiatry*, 24 (1971), pp. 532–535. E. Johnson, "Felon Self-Mutilation: Correlate of Stress in Prison," in Danto, *Jail House Blues*, pp. 237–272. Latin inmates, on the other hand, are overrepresented. See: Beto and Claghorn, "Factors Associated with Self-Multilation"; Claghorn and Beto, "Self-Mutilation"; A. Beigel and H. Russell, "Suicidal Behavior in Jail: Prognostic Considerations," in Danto, *Jail House Blues*, pp. 107–117; Fawcett and Marrs, "Suicide at County Jail." Some of these authors erroneously assume their findings reflect a disproportionate rate of suicide among incarcerated blacks either because they ignore the high percentage of blacks in the institutional population (Danto) or because they compare institutional rates to outside rates without controlling for age (Espera).

[h]Some studies report an overrepresentation of whites among crisis-prone inmates. See: Danto, "Suicide at Wayne County Jail"; Espera, "Attempted and Committed Suicide"; Rieger, "Suicide in Federal Prison." Other studies show that white inmates are proportionately reflected in the self-mutilation group. See Beigel and Russell, "Suicidal Behavior in Jail"; Johnson, "Felon Self-Mutilation"; Claghorn and Beto, "Factors Associated with Self-Mutilation"; Beta and Claghorn, "Self-Mutilation."

ences that may help place their prison breakdowns in context. White inmates are also subdivided into categories that reflect shared cultural experiences and may reveal special susceptibilities to prison pressure.

Notes

1. G. Sykes, *The Society of Captives* (New York: Atheneum, 1966), p. 64.

2. Sykes, *Society of Captives,* chapter 4.

3. Sykes, *Society of Captives,* p. 63. I. Goffman, *Asylums: Essays on the Social Situation of Mental Patients and Other Inmates* (New York: Doubleday & Company, Inc., 1961), p. 43.

4. Sykes, *Society of Captives,* chapter 4. I. Goffman, *Asylums,* p. 43.

5. Sykes, *Society of Captives,* pp. 106-108.

6. Sykes, *Society of Captives,* p. 101.

7. F. Dostoyevsky, *The House of the Dead* (New York: Dell Publishing Company, 1959), p. 34.

8. A. Solzhenitsyn, *The First Circle* (New York: Harper and Row, Publishers, 1968), p. 229.

9. See, for example, Dostoyevsky, *House of Dead,* pp. 37-38, and Sykes, *Society of Captives,* p. 101.

10. S. Wolf and H. Ripley, "Reactions among Allied Prisoners of War Subjected to Three Years of Imprisonment," *American Journal of Psychiatry,* 104 (1947), pp. 85, 180-193.

11. H. Toch, *Men in Crisis: Human Breakdowns in Prison* (Chicago: Aldine Publishing Company, 1975), p. 6.

12. Toch, *Men in Crisis,* p. 6.

13. B. Bettelheim, *The Informed Heart* (New York: Free Press of Glencoe, 1960), pp. 170-171.

14. Solzhenitsyn, *First Circle,* p. 187.

15. T. Morris and P. Morris, *Pentonville: A Sociological Study of an English Prison* (London: Routledge and Kegan Paul, 1963).

16. C. Goshen, "Transcultural Studies: A State Prison Population of Youthful Offenders," *Adolescence,* 4, No. 15 (1969), pp. 401-430.

17. J. Gibbs, "Jailing and Stress," in Toch *Men in Crisis,* pp. 144-162; J. Irwin, *The Felon* (Englewood Cliffs, New Jersey: Prentice-Hall, Inc., 1970), pp. 37-41.

18. T. Mathiesen, *The Defenses of the Weak* (London: Tavistock, 1965), p. 138.

19. Mathiesen, *Defenses of the Weak,* pp. 221–225.

20. Irwin, *Felon,* pp. 67–79.

21. Sykes, *Society of Captives.*

22. *Society of Captives,* p. 105.

23. Gibbs, "Jailing and Stress."

24. Toch, *Men in Crisis,* p. 15.

25. See D. Jones, "The Dangerousness of Imprisonment" (Ph.D. dissertation, School of Criminal Justice, State University of New York at Albany, 1975).

26. J. Genet, Introduction, *Soledad Brother: The Prison Letters of George Jackson* (New York: Bantam Books, 1970), p. 3.

27. W. Skelton, et al., "Stress in Prison," in *A Handbook of Correctional Psychiatry,* I (1968); E. Johnson, "Sociology of Confinement," *Journal of Criminal Law, Criminology and Police Science,* 51 (1961); E. Hamburger, "The Penitentiary and Paranoia," *Corrective Psychiatry and Journal of Social Therapy,* 13, No. 4 (1967), pp. 225–230; A. Davis, "Sexual Assaults in the Philadelphia Prison System and Sheriff's Vans," *Trans-Action,* December 1968, pp. 8–16; D. Jones, "The Dangerousness of Imprisonment" (Ph.D. dissertation, School of Criminal Justice, State University of New York at Albany, 1975).

28. Sykes, *Society of Captives,* p. 80; Irwin, *Felon,* p. 68.

29. Toch, *Men in Crisis,* pp. 284–285.

30. Bettelheim, *Informed Heart,* pp. 121–122, 185.

31. C. Claghorn and D. Beto, "Self-Mutilation in a Prison Mental Hospital," *Corrective Psychiatry and Journal of Social Therapy,* 13, No. 3 (1967), p. 135.

32. D. Beto and J. Claghorn, "Factors Associated with Self-Mutilation within the Texas Department of Correction," *American Journal of Corrections,* January-February 1968, p. 26.

33. Claghorn and Beto, "Self-Mutilation," p. 136.

2 Culture and Adjustment

Social experience influences the degree to which groups have difficulty adjusting to new environments.[1] The extent to which prior experiences insulate or fail to insulate people from the threats posed by unfamiliar enviornments can in some cases be obvious. For example, the comparatively smooth assimilation of Japanese-Americans suggests that Japanese cultural experiences are compatible with the demands of life in the United States.[a] On the other hand, we find moving accounts of the resourcelessness and vulnerability of primitive men when they have been transplanted into alien modern settings.[2] Statistics on ethnic differences in rates of self-mutilation and suicide (see Chapter 1) suggest that experiences associated with ethnic background may have differential relevance to confinement. These experiences may produce different patterns of adjustment and breakdown in penal institutions.

In this chapter we explore some cultural experiences of Latin, black and white inmates and describe the assumptions such experiences may cause members of each group to hold about the world. Particular emphasis is placed on cultural factors that relate to coping. The compatibility of different social experiences and needs with the demands of prison are discussed, and junctures in which pre-prison learning may prove dysfunctional in penal settings are identified. We see that both the assets and liabilities of culturally linked predispositions may promote stress in prison.

Descriptions of the impact of cultural background run some risk of reflecting cultural stereotypes, or what has been aptly termed "single strand fabrics."[3] Unidimensional models of social experience and personality downplay similarities between groups, sidestep limitations of inference imposed by small between-group differences, and assume that general findings apply equally to every member of the group under study.[4] To reliably spell out differences of significance to prison adjustment (and to avoid oversimplification), our focus is on personal characteristics that are strongly linked to cultural background. Such attributes may reflect distinctive world views, coping strategies and sources of personal

---

[a]Kitano observes that because Japanese cultural norms are similar to middle-class American norms, even marginal Japanese-Americans tend to experience relatively few problems of acculturation. H. Kitano, *Japanese Americans: The Evolution of a Subculture* (Englewood Cliffs, New Jersey: Prentice-Hall, Inc., 1972). See also: W. Caudill, "Japanese-American Personality in Acculturation," *(Genetic Psychology Monographs,* 45 (1952), pp. 3–102; W. Caudill and G. DeVos, "Achievement, Culture and Personality: The Case of the Japanese Americans," *American Anthropologist,* 58 (1956), pp. 1102–1126; W. Caudill and H. Scarr, "Japanese Value Orientations and Culture Change," *Ethnology,* 1 (1962), pp. 53–91.

support. Although characteristics that occur across cultural groups may be discussed, our aim is to pull together a plausible picture of differential socialization, and its impact on differential susceptibility to prison pressure.

Family Dependence

Latin men live in warm, supportive, family-centered worlds.[5] The centrality of the family in the lives of most lower class Latin men is a theme that permeates virtually every scholarly work on the personal impact of Latin cultural experiences. There are also many Latin traditions that reflect the significance of family, prominent among which is the custom of presenting oneself "in the framework of the family" during social intercourse.[6] The personal psychology of Latin men may be deeply influenced by pervasive family attachments; for the typical Latin male, the family is often central to his personality: "Even with respect to identification the Chicano *self* is likely to take second place after the family."[7]

The nurturant, unconditionally loving mother represents the focal figure in Latin families. Her mothering role is likely to be played out with children well after they are grown and have children of their own.[8] This is particularly the case with respect to males, a fact that may be related to the prominence of a mother-son relationship comprised of an "emotionally supportive, martyr-like but controlling mother and a tyrannical but dependent son."[9] Descriptions of this paradigm suggest that Latin mother-son relationships may foster dependency by forging a connection in the mind of the growing male between being a man and being cared for and protected: Although the boy is accorded the status of a "little man" (a machito), he is also closely nurtured by his mother, who views him as helpless and dependent.[10]

The family-centered experiences of Latin men have stable correlates. One such correlate is a veiw of the world as composed of an extended kinship network in which social roles and norms are clear, and in which one can feel needed and secure.[11] The world (like the family) must be structured, and must provide predictable sources of emotional support.[12]

Such family-based assumptions tend to produce adult personalities marked by strong dependency and relational needs.[13] Oscar Lewis, after extensive firsthand contact with Latin families, suggests that these orientations may shape a fundamental axis of Latin life: "Money and material possessions, although important, do not motivate their major decisions. Their deepest need is for love and their life is a relentless search for it."[14]

The development and maintenance of the "machismo syndrome"—the Latin image of the manly man—may also be related to the protective role Latin families play for their men. Although characterized by virtues normally reserved for solitary, self-sufficent men—virility, fearlessness, self-control—the "macho" is typically struggling to establish a masculine identity in the face of deep-seated maternal dependency.[15] He is also often the recipient of unquestioning family recognition and support. The relevance of family assistance to the Latin male's view of himself as autonomous and powerful is seen in the manifest (but nonoperative) patriarchial structure of the Latin family—characterized by formal respect and distance accorded to the male—and latent (and operative) matriarchial dominance—featuring strong, low visibility, emotional control of sons by their mothers.[16] Similarly, volatility, expressivity and even unseemly emotional symptoms may be discounted as evidence of personal difficulties and accorded family sympathy.[17] The protective function of the family is particularly evident during periods of crisis, when family members may make a self-conscious effort to shield their man from the implications of failure.[18] Such promiscuous family support and collusion, especially from mothers and wives, may perpetuate a "curious childish quality of adult manhood,"[19] which can conflict with norms (such as the norm of manliness) prevalent in some non-Latin settings.

Although the Latin family may create problems with respect to some non-Latin versions of manhood, it is responsive to demands of its environment. Crises that arise in the Latin world may be successfully reinterpreted or endured with comforting support of family. And many norms in Latin culture dovetail with predispositions spawned in the family and complement the family's ameliorative role. Thus norms that dictate an emphasis on the uniqueness of the individual may offer the prospect of special care and handling for overly dependent and vulnerable men;[20] the focus on tact and diplomacy may provide a shield against flagrant or undue insults to fragile male egos;[21] widespread adulation of the Latin mother may provide a socially acceptable defense against recognition of suffocating maternal dependency.[22] Moreover, the Latin tendency to view ideals—such as love, justice, and loyalty—abstractly rather than operationally may be comforting,[23] though it may lead to flagrantly selective perception. Propositions rarely tested tend to become increasingly troublesome working assumptions. Looking the other way may save face, insure tranquility, and ward off feelings of insecurity, but it does so only as long as the supports that sustain the fiction are operative.

Incarceration may pose unavoidable tests of the Latin man's world view, his family status, and his self-image. Such tests can prove disturbing and crisis promotive.

Dependency and Prison Stress

A Latin background seems to create susceptibilities to problems of confinement. We have noted that crises involving self-mutilation and attempted suicide are disproportionately prevalent among Latin prisoners (Chapter 1). The Latin males' difficulty in handling confinement suggests a lack of fit between his family-centered dependency orientation and the survival requirements of prison.

Prisons may dramatize problems Latins faced in immigrating and settling in this country. Although assimilation may have proven stressful for many Latin-Americans, the demands of adjustment to prison arise when the Latin male is apart from his family, which is his major source of identity and emotional support. Many confined men may find the separation from family painful, and may have difficulty adjusting to prison norms. For some, letters and visits from loved ones may help reduce the pains of prison, as may the security of knowing that there is a family to return to on release. Others may find support from members of extended kinship groups (or from friends of relatives) who are also confined. Davidson, for example, observes that Chicano kin may sometimes play the role of a "mother," providing aid for "her child through the long process of enculturation" to prison.[24] Some militant Chicano groups, loosely included under the rubric "Family" in California penal institutions, may provide a supportive context in which a man's "machismo" rests assured.[25]

For some Latin convicts, however, prison survival may hinge on the integrity of their family ties, rather than on their personal resourcefulness or on the availiability of sibling-like peers. Both jails and prisons can aggravate a Latin man's insecurities regarding his family ties because they offer a substantial number of cues to abandonment.[b] Some Latin men may be unable to survive in the absence of family support, or in settings that differ so radically from their home environments. Because prisons may not offer acceptable alternative sources of support for family-dependent inmates, these men find themselves resourceless.

Ghetto Socialization

The social experiences of lower class blacks differ sharply in many respects from those to which Latin men are typically exposed. Black culture, rooted in the violence and oppression of the antebellum South, reflects a strong concern for survival in a hostile world.[26] Salient themes and orientations to life, paraphrased as "soul" and "making it," are steeped in the image of a threatening world, and prize the qualities of resourcefulness and endurance.[27]

Survival techniques developed in response to slave and caste status involved the maintenance of a defensive, self-protectively vigilant posture, coupled with the concealment of feelings (particularly anger and fear) behind a facade of obsequiousness or serenity.[28]

Residues of such concerns and techniques have been described by various

[b]Major cues to strained or broken ties to significant others include unexplained delays of mail and/or cancellation of visits. Some prison researchers note that the social isolation of penal institutions can make a man overly concerned with family ties. See J. Irwin, *The Felon* (Englewood Cliffs, New Jersey: Prentice-Hall, Inc., 1970), and J. Gibbs (Doctoral Prospectus, School of Criminal Justice, SUNYA, 1974) for works that highlight the role of family-related cues and stresses for jail inmates.

students of modern-day ghetto blacks. Grier and Cobbs tell us that "a Black norm has developed—a suspiciousness of one's environment which is necessary for survival," and similar observations have been made by a number of other authors.[29]

Mood-masking strategies—the norm of "playing it cool"—differ from the strategy of not showing feelings that could earn serious punishment. Whereas the "Uncle Tom" pose was directed at whites and was meant to convey servility or harmlessness, the cool role of the ghetto is directed primarily to peers, and conveys the image of someone who is smooth and "together," yet also hard, cold and potentially explosive.[30] But both facades are meant to put people off, to avoid victimization, and to hide self-revealing ("uncool") feelings of anger or fear.

The common thread running thought black postures and styles is not merely a continuation of a caste mentality, or the legacy of slavery. Rather, such adaptations reflect the continuing experiences of ghetto residents. Lee Rainwater, an astute observer of slum life and an able sociohistorian, suggests that ghetto blacks are exposed to fundamentally the same presures as their slave predecessors. To survive, poor blacks must now (as then) assume the pose of victim:

The cultural mechanisms which Negroes had developed for living the life of victim continued to be serviceable as the victimization process was maintained (after emancipation) first under the myths of white supremacy and black inferiority, later by the doctrine of gradualism which covered the fact of no improvement in position, and finally by the modern Northern system of ghettoization and indifference.[31]

Cast in the role of victim, sealed off from conventional society, ghetto blacks often victimize and exploit each other and help to create environments marked by constant uncertainity. Special skills must be developed to survive such pressures. The ability to avoid or escape unnecessary and unmanageable situations must be complemented by the readiness to deal with such situations when they arise. "I walk my walk and talk my talk" (I mind my own business), and "shucking and jiving" (talking your way out of trouble) are means of avoiding danger.[32] The need to flee in the face of overwhelming threat is a recognized and respected option.[33] These strategies require considerable sophistication and "cool." If they are not carried off with aplomb, they may backfire, signalling lameness, weakness or cowardice.

Training to survive the threats of ghetto life begins early—in families where victimization "prepares and toughens its members to function in the ghetto world," and in slum streets where children learn norms of violence as routine features of play.[34] Young men become concerned with the issue of personal safety and begin to cultivate early the rudiments of the ghetto's "hard man" image.[35] Given his inhospitable environment, the ghetto man must also internalize an expectation of trouble, hurt and duplicity. He must remain alert to the possibility of deception and abuse, to the ubiquitous ghetto art of "gaming."[36] Fellow men are therefore treated cautiously and viewed with suspicion and distrust, since most of life's games, and particularly those that may prove harmful, involve other men.

A ghetto man may emerge from his daily encounters physically unharmed, in possession of his money and with his self-esteem intact. But he may yet encounter the law, because ghetto activities are apt to be of marginal legality. Hanging with one's street-corner peers, for example, is routine ghetto fare. Such conduct, however, exposes men to a variety of quasi-legitimate and illegitimate busts, the culmination of which involves arrest for what one slum dweller termed "suspicion of suspicion."[37] While such a comment may reflect subcultural humor, it may also reveal a reality for many ghetto men, who come to feel that they are pawns in a massive state conspiracy to withhold aid or to intervene and stunt their lives.[38]

The pressures of ghetto life, it may be argued, encourage social isolation as a means to avoid trouble. But the feeling that threat is endemic and unscheduled may more often leave a person feeling that safety can be found in numbers. Though distrust toward strangers and police is rife, a strong (functional) peer orientation among many urban low income blacks results. There is a romantic "loyalty" to "street buddies" who can be counted on in times of crisis.[39] It is of course true that many ghetto men feel they must ultimately be prepared to "go it alone," since slum life breeds shifting and impermanent liaisons, or may establish superficial links to peers for the sole purpose of avoiding danger. But peer support, in the final analysis, represents a highly valued resource in this turbulent world, where every man ultimately requires an audience responsive to ghetto definitions of manhood and personal worth.[40]

Ghetto survival is characterized by emphasis on self-protection in a cold, unpredictable, often hostile world, where the most reliable source of support can be found among similarly circumstanced peers. Incarceration is one of the hazards life has to offer and penal settings pose tests on which ghetto experiences may be brought to bear—and for which they prove functional.

Ghetto and Prison

Blacks have low rates of self-destructive behavior in penal settings, as noted in Chapter 1. The source of this relative resilience may lie in the close fit of ghetto survival norms to the survival requirements of prison.

A ghetto background may give a man an edge in confinement because ghetto and prison share a number of important characteristics. For one, both settings are peer centered, unpredictable and dangerous, and explicitly attuned to the issue of surviving. Both settings reward an image of manliness that features traits of strength, forebearance and courage. Conventional indices of status and manliness are scarce in both settings, which creates a premium on supportive peer groups and on formalized procedures for the stigmatizing of susceptible men. Moreover, in both the ghetto and the prison, survival concerns are reinforced by the presence of social control agents who sometimes pose challenges and threats.

Focal ghetto concerns of survival, toughness and resilience approximate the prison's image of the "real" or "manly man." Black folklore heroes are modelled on premises similar to that of the "manly man." There is a close association between ancient and modern folklore tricksters (Brier Rabbit, the Monkey) and the modern-day cool role, and between historical and current folklore models of hardness and strength (the "bad nigger," Stagolee) and the ideal of the man who remains unmoved by pressure.[41] Coolness and strength, although dichotimized in folklore, are "facets of a single if somewhat amorphous conception of ghetto-specific masculinity," which dictates a flexible balance of brain and brawn.[42] Prisons and jails reinforce the stance of coolness (and its peer orientation) and honor its claim.

In stressing the relevance of ghetto experiences to penal settings, we do not imply that the experience of confinement will be stress free for black convicts. The mandate of the cool role, as one popular blues song has it, requires a man to "ride with the tide and go with the flow." But we have noted that many ghetto men may view the criminal justice system and its agents with suspicion. Various features of penal institutions can enhance a man's sense of himself as a victim of arbitrary and unjust treatment.[c] Feelings of powerlessness and resentment should be manageable for many confined blacks, however, because ghettos equip men to play the victim role. Strategic declarations of injustice (censoriousness) can prove functional in prison; they make the inmate seem less blameworthy and may even influence staff conduct, thus providing evidence of fate control. Attributing blame to others may also help a person deal with long-term problems of personal worth. The ghetto man may appear handicapped in settings that feature middle class norms, where he assesses his accomplishments by conventional standards.[d] But failure to achieve economic or social success may have reduced impact where inmates see incarceration (and attendant complications, such as lost jobs or unfulfilled obligations) as an arbitrary intervention over which they have little control. While such events spawn bitterness and anger, they absolve the "victim" of responsibility for his fate.[e]

We know that there are persons who have been traumatized by ghetto experiences. Ghettos, like prisons, force some men to play demeaning roles so that

---

[c]The pains of prison that emerge as threats to a man's autonomy may play into these susceptibilities, not the least of which are arbitrary (or unexplained) decisions made by criminal justice personnel. See G. Sykes, *The Society of Captives* (New Jersey: Princeton University Press, 1959), and T. Mathiesen, *The Defenses of the Weak* (London: Tavistock, 1965).

[d]E. Liebow (*Tally's Corner* [Boston: Little, Brown and Co., 1967]) observes that such invidious comparisons caused some pain for many of the street corner blacks he studied.

other, stronger men, may affirm their masculinity. Although prisons may be objectively less dangerous than slum streets for skilled denizens of the ghetto, whom incarceration protects from more lethal encounters,[43] the problem of survival for susceptible men may be more salient in confinement than in the ghetto. Games of peer emasculation, for example, are more prevalent and insidious in prison.[44] These games may require more finesse and "cool" than their ghetto counterparts. And in confinement men are more directly subject to official control than they are in the ghetto. Such conditions may prove crisis promotive for a few blacks because their ghetto experience, unlike that of most black convicts, has left them doubtful and afraid, hypersensitive to hints of violence and threat.[f] Prisons may amplify such doubts and fears, and make it difficult or impossible to avoid danger.

Lack of fit between one's resources and survival norms can often be disguised in the free coummunity. Here, the citizen has more command over his world. Within limits, he is free to select his environments, schedule his encounters, cross (or fail to cross) bridges of his choosing. Prisons are less accommodating. The confined man is measured in terms of the manliness norm of prison, and discrepancies between a man and this model are likely to be noted. For men for whom discretion has been the substance of valor, institutional testing grounds may spell failure and defeat. The conditons created by the prison "manliness myth" may thus highlight impotence and vulnerability and leave the victims of the ghetto feeling trapped and resourceless, devoid of peer support.

Our descriptions of Latin and black cultural experiences stress configurations of traits, values and norms that typify groups with common problems. They are not meant to suggest that such conditions are intrinsic to any ethnic group, or that they are uniformly distributed. Some Latin men become deeply enmeshed in street life, and may show a corresponding decrease (or temporary suspension) of family dependence; others may be particularly close to their families.[g] Similarly, there may be ghetto blacks who maintain close links to family and are relatively uninvolved in slum social life, or who seem able to straddle peer and family-centered worlds; some may be considerably more street-oriented (and street wise) than their peers.[h]

---

[e]Much of black political prisoner ideology, for example, seems designed to neutralize the threats incarceration might pose to man's self-esteem. See G. Jackson, *Soledad Brother: The Prison Letters of George Jackson* (New York: Bantam Books, 1970) and A. Davis, *If They Come in the Morning* (New York: Signet Books, 1971).

[f]The reactions of traumatized ghetto blacks may be analogous to the syndrome typical of persons who undergo serious "near-miss" disaster episodes. Such persons become hypervigilant because *"anticipations of personal invulnerability are so completely shattered* that [they are] no longer able to ward off strong reflective fear when [they] encounter new danger cues."* R. Lazarus, *Psychological Stress and the Coping Process* (New York: McGraw-Hill, Inc., 1966), p. 110.

Some nonmodal coping patterns may differentially influence the shape of prison stress. A Latin who abandons his family for the streets may be prone to experience remorse after he is confined because incarceration may bring home to him how much pain his delinquent activities have caused loved ones. A black convict concerned about family ties may feel the sting of victimization all the more intensely because he may feel that his arrest represents an effort on the part of the criminal justice system to prevent him from being with and caring for his family; a fearful inmate may feel more vulnerable and alone if family ties prove unstable. The issue of the differential relevance of less uniform preprison experiences may be particularly germaine in viewing the susceptibilities of the comparatively diverse group represented by white Americans.

Residual Coping Patterns

The social experiences of white Americans — our residual category — are variable and difficult to describe. The impact of such experiences is likewise hard to assess. However, we know that some white subcultures must generate concerns that overlap with those linked to the cultural experiences of Latin and black men. White men from stable working or middle class homes, for example, are likely to exhibit a strong family orientation, in the same category as that of Latin men. The poor white male, like his minority counterpart, should be responsive to lower class "focal concerns."[45] Whites with extensive criminal and street experience may share with blacks a heightened concern for survival, duplicity and the impermanence of relationships. Farm or small town whites may be exposed to social environments comparable in essential respects to those experienced by Latin men.[46]

Comparatively few white men, however, may experience formative environments that yield concerns for family ties or personal survival as salient as those associated with Latin families and black ghettos. With the exception of rural Appalachian whites[47] (whose extreme poverty and social isolation enhance family ties) and some first-generation American immigrants (particularly

---

[g]Piri Thomas, for example, in his book *Down These Mean Streets* (New York: Signet Books, 1967), provides an autobiographical account of a Latin male with strong peer and family ties. These relationships took precedence at different times. J. Fitzpatrick *(Puerto Rican Americans: The Meaning of Migration to the Mainland* (Englewood Cliffs, New Jersey: Prentice-Hall, Inc., 1971) notes that younger Latins may show stronger family ties than adults, but some may also rebel against family controls and establish street loyalties.

[h]Claude Brown, for example, notes in *Manchild in the Promised Land* (New York: Signet Books, 1965), that some of his peers progressed more deeply than others into ghetto street life, and a few established quasi-conventional lives. Many blacks, according to L. Rainwater *(Behind Ghetto Walls* [Chicago: Aldine Publishing Company, 1970]) try to maintain family and street lives. But street norms often make marriages unstable. Thus, many ghetto men end up investing the bulk of their time and psychic energies in male-centered street activities.

Itlaians),[48] no white subcultural group appears to display a family orientation as central and encompassing as that described for Latin men. Although it is true that recent ethnic immigrants generally rely on their families to survive culture shock, this reaction seems particularly marked among Puerto Rican and Mexican-Americans.[49] The fact that migration tends to be two-way for Latin-Americans, in contrast to the traditional one-way pattern of European immigrants, may accentuate ethnic group and family attachments in the lives of these men.[50]

Similarly, some lower class focal concerns may be uniquely manifested among ghetto dwellers. Black slum residents must cope with racial bias in addition to class discrimination. This "double deprivation" may result in unique connotations accorded to some lower class concerns.[51] Thus, the issue of survival in an inhospitable world may be relevant to many lower class men (regardless of ethnic group), but this theme seems particularly marked among ghetto blacks, who occupy (or feel they occupy) an especially vulnerable position in American society.[52]

More generally, slum blacks often "look" less lower class than poor whites. Low income white neighborhoods tend to be more stable than minority areas; and the perspectives and behavior of lower class whites show a more substantial influence of middle class values, norms and aspirations.[53] For example, research reveals that whites in Chicago slums, in contrast to ghetto blacks, are typically less peer and street oriented, more prone to participate in traditional organizations (such as churches or clubs), and more intimately tied to extended kinship groups. Street corner activities and crime emerged "almost imperceptibly" from mainstream ghetto norms. Equivalent conduct in lower class white communities, on the other hand, had the connotation of rebellion against established norms, and often resulted in the person's finding himself in open conflict with the larger community.[54] Ultimately, a high proportion of delinquents may respond to such community pressures and adopt more conventional life-styles.[55]

Since relatively few low income whites may populate the ranks of the "hard core" or "unstable" poor, they may be less likely than slum blacks to show pronounced lower class behavior patterns. A sizeable number of low income whites may be classified as "sheltered," "pampered," or "middle class" by ghetto and prison standards. These men may originate in relatively stable lower or working class neighborhoods and may adhere to middle class norms and values. Imprisonment, and the roles that must be played to survive in prison, may prove unfamiliar to them. The prison experience may seem particularly alien and threatening to less street wise men. Unaquainted with prison norms, bereft of social status and family support, such men may find themselves susceptible to a wide range of pressures that reflect their marginal status in the prison community.

Summary

We have suggested that many Latin and black inmates should respond to prison in a manner that reflects culturally determined world views and coping strategies

Table 2-1
Summary of Observations about Cultural Differences and the Relevance of Culturally Linked Experiences to Confinement

Social Experience Group	Congruence with the Prison Survival Model (Manly Man)	Adjustment Difficulties in Confinement (Inferred from Rates of Self-injury)	Locus of Adjustment Difficulties	Locus of Adjustment Crises
Family dependence (Latins)				
World view—stable, warm, family-centered	Low	High	Family support	Family support
Response—overt relationship seeking, premised on expression of support needs	Low			
Source of support—family	Low			
Ghetto socialization (blacks)				
World view—unpredictable, dangerous, male-centered	High	Low	Victimization-resentment	Fear
Response—suspicion, self-protective stance, overlaid by cool exterior	High			
Source of support—peers	High			
Residual category (whites)				
World view—variable	Variable	Variable	Variable	Variable
Response—variable	Variable			
Source of support—variable	Variable			

(see Table 2-1). Each perspective is relevant to the demands posed in its natural or formative environment. Latin family-centered experiences should be disproportionately productive of difficulties. Ghetto experiences seem relevant to confinement, though not for men who are casualties of the slum. For white prisoners, the expectation is that reactions to prison stress will vary substantially, depending upon preprison social experience. Subgroups defined in terms of such variables as social class, age and criminal career may yield distinctive patterns of prison adjustment.

Notes

1. Relevant studies include: R. Schermerhorn, "The Polish American" in R. Schermerhorn (Ed.), *These, Our People: Minorities in the American Culture* (Boston: D.C. Heath and Company, 1949), pp. 265-290; L. Doob, "An Introduction to the Psychology of Acculturation," *Journal of Social Psychology,* 45 (1957), pp. 143-360; A. Cohen, *Delinquent Boys* (New York: Macmillan, 1955); E. Vogt, "Navaho Veternas: A Study of Changing Values," *Peabody Museum Papers,* 41 No. 1 (1951); B. Bettelheim, *The Informed Heart* (New York: Free Press of Glencoe, 1960). See generally: A. Hallowell, "Ojibwa Personality and Acculturation," in S. Tax (Ed.), *Acculturation in the Americas* (Chicago: University of Chicago Press, 1952), pp. 105-112; D. Kennedy, "Key Issues in the Cross-Cultural Study of Mental Disorders," in B. Kaplan (Ed.), *Studying Personality Cross-Culturally* (Evanston, Ill.: Row and Peterson, 1961), pp. 405-426; Stouffer et al., *The American Soldier: Adjustment During Army Life* (Princeton: Princeton University Press, 1949).

2. See, for example, Tax, *Acculturation in Americas.*

3. E. Herzog, "Social Sterotypes and Social Research," *Journal of Social Issues,* 26, No. 3 (1970), pp. 109-125, p. 116.

4. Herzog, "Social Stereotypes," pp. 116-117.

5. J. Fitzpatrick, *Puerto Rican Americans: The Meaning of Migration to the Mainland* (Englewood Cliffs, New Jersey: Prentice-Hall, Inc., 1971), pp. 78-79. See also: J. Gillin, "Ethos Components in Modern Latin American Culture" *American Anthropologist,* 68, No. 1 (1955), pp. 488-500; W. Madsen, "Mexican-Americans and Anglo-Americans: A Comparative Study of Mental Health in Texas," in S. Plog and R. Edgerton (Eds.), *Changing Perspectives in Mental Illness* (New York: Holt, Rinehart and Winston, 1969), pp. 217-251.

6. Fitzpatrick, *Puerto Rican Americans,* pp. 78-79.

7. N. Murillo, "The Mexican American Family," in N. Wagner and M. Haur. (Eds.), *Chicanos: Social and Psychological Perspectives* (St. Louis: C.V. Mosley, 1971), pp. 97-102.

8. Murillo, "Mexican Family," p. 104.

9. L. Rogler and A. Hollingshead, *Trapped: Families and Schizophrenia*

(New York: John Wiley & Sons, Inc., 1965), p. 312. Also see: K. Wolf, "Growing Up and Its Price in Three Puerto Rican Sub-Cultures," *Psychiatry,* 15, No. 4 (1952), pp. 401–433; S. Mintz, "An Essay in the Definition of National Culture," in F. Cordasco and E. Bricchione (Eds.), *The Puerto Rican Experience* Totowa, New Jersey: Rowman & Littlefield, 1973), pp. 26–90; O. Lewis, *La Vida: A Puerto Rican Family in the Culture of Poverty, San Juan and New York* (New York: Vintage Books, 1965); D. Guerrero, "Neurosis and the Mexican Family Structure," *American Journal of Psychiatry,* 112, (1955), pp. 411–417; D. Guerrero, *Psychology of the Mexican: Culture and Personality* (Austin: University of Texas Press, 1975); R. Fernandez-Marina, E. Maldonado-Sierra, and R. Trent, "Three Basic Themes in Mexican and Puerto Rican Family Values," *Journal of Social Psychology,* 49 (1958), pp. 167–181.

10. Rogler and Hollingshead, *Trapped,* p. 312.

11. Murillo, "Mexican Family," p. 99.

12. Fitzpatrick, *Puerto Rican Americans,* p. 90.

13. See: V. Petrullo, Puerto Rican Paradox (Philadelphia: University of Pennsylvania Press, 1947); J. Brown, "Subcultures of Isolation in Rural Puerto Rico," in Cordasco and Bricchione (Eds.), *Puerto Rican Experience;* M. Albizer, C. Marty-Torress, and H. Marty-Torress, "Atisbos de la Personalidad Puertoriguena" (Attributes of the Puerto Rican Personality), *Resista de Cienceas Sociales,* 2, No. 3 (1958), pp. 120–132.

14. Lewis, *La Vida,* p. XXX.

15. M. Maccoby, "On Mexican National Character," in Wagner and Haur (Eds.), *Chicanos,* pp. 123–131.

16. S. Minuchin et al., *Families of the Slums* (New York: Basic Books, Inc., 1967).

17. A. Rubel, "Concepts of Disease in Mexican-American Culture," *American Anthropologist,* 62 (1960), pp. 795–814; A. Rubel, "The Epidemiology of a Folk Illness: Susto in Hispanic America," *Ethnology,* 3 (1964), pp. 268–283.

18. Madsen, "Mexican-Americans and Anglo-Americans," p. 239.

19. Mintz, "National Culture," p. 75.

20. Fitzpatrick, *Puerto Rican Americans.*

21. Murillo, "Mexican Family"; O. Paz, *The Labyrinthes of Solitude: Life and Thought in Mexico* (New York: Grove Press, 1961).

22. Maccoby, "Mexican Character," p. 123.

23. Fitzpatrick, *Puerto Rican Americans.*

24. R. T. Davidson, *Chicano Prisoners: The Key to San Quentin* (New York: Holt, Rinehart and Winston, 1974), p. 21.

25. Davidson, *Chicano Prisoners,* p. 84.

26. L. Singer, "Ethnogenesis and Negro-Americans Today," *Social Re-*

search, 29 (1962), pp. 419-432; W. Phillips, "Survival Techniques of Black Americans," in R. Goldstein (Ed.) *Black Life and Culture* (New York: Coswell Co., 1960).

27. R. Blauner, "Black Culture: Lower Class Result or Ethnic Creation?" in L. Rainwater (Ed.), *Soul* (New Brunswick, New Jersey: Transaction, Inc., 1970), pp. 129-156.

28. A. Pettigrew, *A Profile of the Negro-American* (New Jersey: D. Van Nostrand, 1964); H. Finestone, "Cats, Kicks and Color," *Social Problems,* 5 (1957), pp. 3-14; W. Grier and P. Cobbs, *Black Rage* (New York: Basic Books, 1968).

29. Grier and Cobbs, *Black Rage,* p. 172; A. Kardiner and L. Ovesey, *The Mark of Oppression: Explorations in the Personality of the American Negro* (New York: W.W. Norton & Company, Inc., 1951); G. Suttles, *The Social Order of the Slum* (Chicago: University of Chicago Press, 1968); E. Baughman, *Black Americans* (New York: Academic Press, 1971); Pettigrew, *Profile of Negro Americans;* H. R. Cayton, "The Psychology of the Negro under Discrimination," in A. Rose (Ed.), *Race Prejudice and Discrimination* (New York: Springer Publsihing Company, 1958).

30. Suttles, *Social Order of Slum*; U. Hannerz, *Soulside* (New York: Columbia University Press, 1969).

31. L. Rainwater, "Crucible of Identify: The Negro Lower Class Family," *Daedalus,* 95, No. 1 (Winter 1966), pp. 172-216, 174. See generally: L. Rainwater, *Behind Ghetto Walls* (Chicago: Aldine Publishing Company, 1970) and Blauner, "Black Culture."

32. Hannerz, *Soulside.*

33. E. Liebow, *Tally's Corner* (Boston: Little, Brown and Co., 1967).

34. Rainwater, "Crucible," p. 176.

35. Alan Sutter, "Playing a Cold Game: Phases of a Ghetto Career," *Urban Life and Culture,* April 1972, pp. 77-91, p. 79; C. Brown, *Manchild in the Promised Land* (New York: Signet Books, 1965).

36. Hannerz, *Soulside*, p. 146. See also H. Toch, "The Delinquent as Poor Loser," *Seminars in Psychiatry,* 3 (1971), pp. 386-399, and Liebow, *Tally's Corner.*

37. J. Horton, "Time and Cool People," *Tranaction,* 4 (April 1967), pp. 5-12, p. 7.

38. Sutter, "Playing Cold Game," p. 83.

39. Hannerz, *Soulside*

40. Ibid.

41. R. Abrahams, *Deep Down in the Jungle* (Pennsylvania: Folklore Associates, 1964).

42. Hannerz, *Soulside.*

43. D. Jones, "The Dangerousness of Imprisonment" (Ph.D. dissertation, State University of New York at Albany, 1975), chapter 4.

44. H. Toch, *Men in Crisis: Human Breakdowns in Prison* (Chicago: Aldine Publishing Company, 1975).

45. W. Miller, "Lower Class Culture as a Generating Milieu of Gang Delinquency," *Journal of Social Issues,* 14, No. 3 (1958), pp. 5-19.

46. See M. Beiser, "A Study of Personality Assets in a Rural Community," *Archives of General Psychiatry,* 24 (1971), pp. 249-253; W. Warner et al., *Yankee City* (New Haven and London: Yale University Press, 1963); G. Summers, L. Seiler, and R. Hough, "Psychiatric Symptoms: Cross Validation with a Rural Sample," *Rural Sociology,* 36 (1971), pp. 374-378, p. 377.

47. J. Finney, "Intercultural Differences in Personality," in J. Finney (Ed.), *Culture Change, Mental Health and Poverty* (New York: Simon and Schuster, 1969), pp. 234-274.

48. L. Barzini, *Italian Americans* (New York: Atheneum, 1964).

49. Fitzpatrick, *Puerto Rican Americans;* L. Strole et al., *Mental Health in the Metropolis: The Midtown Manhattan Study* (New York: McGraw-Hill, Inc., 1961).

50. Lewis, *La Vida.*

51. Rainwater, *Ghetto Walls;* Blauner, "Black Culture."

52. Blauner, "Black Culture," p. 150.

53. Rainwater, *Ghetto Walls;* J. Short and F. Strodbeck, *Group Process and Gang Delinquency* (Chicago: The University of Chicago Press, 1965).

54. Short and Strodbeck, *Group Process,* pp. 102-115.

55. See W. F. Whyte, *Street Corner Society: The Social Structure of an Italian Slum* (Chicago: The University of Chicago Press, 1943), p. 272.; and F. Thrasher, "The Gang," in M. Clinard and R. Quinney, *Criminal Behavior Systems: A Typology* (New York: Holt, Rinehart and Winston, Inc., 1967), pp. 336-341, p. 340, a reprint of sections of Thrasher, *The Gang: A Study of 1,313 Gangs in Chicago* (Chicago: The University of Chicago Press, 1927).

3 Method of Inquiry

The data for this book stem from a three year study of self-mutilation and attempted suicide in New York State penal institutions.[a] A semistructured clinical interview conducted with a sample of self-destructive inmates and a sample of non-self-destructive inmates was the major research tool used in the project. Available background and criminal career information was also collected about inmates with recorded incidents of self-injury and on comparison samples drawn from the relevant populations.

The penal institutions surveyed fall into two categories: a prison sample, which consists of all New York State maximum security institutions, and a jail sample, which included three major New York City pretrial detention facilities.[b] Both the prison and jail samples are comprised of one or more facilities that house adults, adolescents, and men with diagnosed psychiatric difficulties. The prison sample covers eight out of every ten sentenced felons in New York State.[1] The jail sample is not as comprehensive, because access to other detention settings was unobtainable. But the jails studied include what was the most populous New York City detention center for adults during the period of research, all pretrial adolescents in New York City, and a major facility for suicidal jail inmates.[2] Prison inmates who experienced jail crises provide additional cases for the detention sample, and include examples of breakdowns that occurred in other New York City jails, as well as in upstate county jails.

The analysis of ethnic patterns of self-destructive behavior in confinement focuses on interviews conducted with crisis-prone Latin, black and white inmates. Also interviewed from the three ethnic categories was a random sample of inmates who did not have recorded incidents of self-mutilation while confined; this sample serves as a comparison group. Population figures and survey data for the prisons are used to describe the relative prevalence of breakdown among members of different cultural groups and to explore the differential distribution of content themes derived from the interviews.

---

[a]Studies of Inmate Self-Destruction (R01 MH 20696). This project was funded by the National Institute of Mental Health, Washington, D. C., and directed by Hans Toch.

[b]The prisons surveyed include: Attica, Auburn, Clinton, Eastern, Elmira, Coxsackie, Great Meadows, Green Haven, Ossining (Sing-Sing), and Dannemore (now Matteawan) State Hospital. The jails studied were: Manhattan House of Detention for Men, Riker's Island Adolescent Remand Shelter, and Riker's Island Hospital.

Our index of crisis is physically self-destructive conduct. Other measures of stress are available, so the rationale for use of this index warrants discussion.

Our focus on self-injury crisis reflects a number of considerations. For one, prison breakdowns featuring self-mutilation and attempted suicide serve as a self-defined universe for study of groups at risk. Such crises may be useful measures of prison stress because they are disproportionately prevalent in confinement. Although reliable figures are hard to find, available indicators suggest that self-mutilation has reached epidemic proportions in prison.[3] Self-destructive conduct also overlaps (statistically) with other available indices of prison coping failures, including mental health commitments, requests for protective custody, and staff perceptions of inmate crises.[c] Prisoners who characterize themselves as undergoing stressful experiences also use self-destructive thoughts and impulses to document their discomfort.[4]

Self-destructive crises may also provide a more comprehensive picture of the concerns associated with prison breakdowns than other available measures. Any exploration of crises that lead to mental commitments overrepresents psychotic themes.[5] Crises indexed by prisoner requests for protective housing or by observations of prison staff produce a portrait of stress that emphasizes fear or family-related themes.[6] Self-injury crises, by contrast, reflect a wide range of motives and concerns. These breakdowns also encompass a broad spectrum of crisis-prone subjects, from persons who fall victim to specific types of situational pressure to these who would be categorized as highly brittle and psychotic.[7] Findings derived from analysis of self-destructive breakdowns are thus likely to be reasonably representative of inmates in crisis and of the stresses of prison.

The Personal Meaning of Stress

The goal of this study was to portray as fully and accurately as possible the sources of human despair in prison and to trace their cultural antecedents. To this end, we conducted exploratory, person-centered interviews with a sample of 325 men for whom the prison experience had proven overwhelming. We sought descriptions of the shape of each man's crisis, and of the factors that contributed to breakdown. We also interviewed 146 randomly selected inmates, who had coped more effectively with prison stress, to assess the generalizability of our findings with self-destructive men.

---

[c]Thirty-eight percent of patients admitted to the New York State prison mental health facility over a continuous nine-month interval had histories of self-inflicted injury while confined (Hans Toch, *Men in Crisis: Human Breakdowns in Prison* [Chicago: Aldine Publishing Company, 1975], p. 128); 45 percent of protective self-segregation cases in New York State prisons have histories of institutional self-mutilation (Daniel Lockwood, "Protection Survey" [unpublished manuscript, 1975]). My own experience interviewing on-line prison personnel about crisis management indicates that 41 percent of the crises encountered by staff involve acts of self-mutilation.

Statistics on sampling are available to the interested reader in Appendix A, which also contains a description of the background information collected from the institutional files of our subjects. Our focus here is on the nature of the interviews and the information they provide on coping and failing to cope in prison. Subsequent chapters are devoted to analysis and exploration of culturally determined susceptibilities revealed in our discussions with men in crisis.

The Crisis Interview

The clinical interview schedule followed with crisis-prone inmates involved the systematic reconstruction of events, feelings, and concerns leading to the self-destructive act. This interview represented the primary method of data collection on prison crises. Modeled on the procedure employed by Hans Toch to explore acts of violence, the interview schedule entails allowing the subject to state in his own words and in chosen sequence the motives and meanings involved in each incident, and as many details as he can remember.[8] This material is then worked through again with the respondent, this time with a step-by-step, sequential ordering.

The interview was focused, in the manner described by Merton and Kendall,[9] but there was no predefined set of questions. The aim was to pursue the incident as it occurred from the respondent's point of view. This procedure remained constant. Minor variations reflect adjustments of the schedule made to accommodate differences among respondents. Some men, for example, gave sparse descriptions of their breakdown(s). The interviewer was then forced to pose some direct questions to establish the context of the crisis prior to sequential reconstruction. Others gave descriptions of coping failures that were vague or confused. Repeated questioning was sometimes required in such cases to determine if the interviewer understood the sequence before continuing with the schedule.

Typical exploratory probes include such open-ended questions as "what seemed to be the problem" or "maybe you can tell me what your situation was" at the time of the incident. Such questions often elicit a skeletal description of the ingredients for the person's crisis. For example:

I: . . . maybe you can give me some idea of what the problem was?

49: It was a long time ago, about 10 months ago. At the time—you are aware that prisons have homosexuality here—I'll put it this way, my mate went home. I call it her and I almost fell in love with her, I could say. That's how much the relationship meant to me. I sort of lost my head because of my feelings for her. I started thinking about that because he went home and I felt sorry for myself, like I lost him. And I felt hurt inside. To me it was one of the worst feelings in the world. See I've never had anybody. And when you meet somebody and you really get to know these people you want to stay with them. I broke up. And I still haven't quite gotten over it. What I did I regret, but I know why I done it.

Follow-up questions aim at a more detailed phenomenological description of the self-destructive event and require the interviewee to reconstruct his thoughts and feelings as his crisis unfolded. The schedule culminates with requests for a detailed description of the person's subjective world just prior to (and sometimes during) the self-destructive act. The interview was thus designed to produce in-depth accounts of personal breakdowns as they were experienced by the man in crisis.[10] (A sample interview is available for inspection in Appendix B.)

Our interviews were premised on the assumption that the personal significance of a man's actions can be directly approached by allowing him to reconstruct his frame of mind at the time of the behavior in question, however obscure or odd this view may currently appear to the person. To capitalize on such information, the interviewer must deal with a man's premises at the time of the incident, however unusual or artificial they may appear, and explore them in depth. There is considerable evidence that motivation for introspection develops when a man is placed in a role that approximates that of a co-researcher into his own difficulties.[11] This may be particularly true for incarcerated men, because penal institutions frequently discourage open consideration of personal problems or susceptibilities.[12] Most of the subjects thus seized the opportunity for detailed exploration presented by the interview. Some claimed that the interviewers were the first people to approach them regarding personal problems created by incarceration. Others described the experience as therapeutic.

The success of the interview approach is confirmed by the relatively low refusal rate (five percent) among self-destructive inmates. The additional fact that black and Latin inmates were as willing to share their concerns as white prisoners is particularly impressive, since minority inmates might feel suspicious when approached by white, middle-class researchers who are armed with tape recorders and official approval for a study of stigma-imbued psychological breakdowns.

The resistance that emerged among minority inmates to being interviewed was sometimes overcome by involving peers as team interviewers or translators, who would help recruit a few of the interview candidates. Such assistance proved invaluable for interviewing Spanish men, and with a few black convicts who were leery of the researchers during the initial phases of the study. Inmate assistants even provided helpful clues about the nature of the problem experienced by some respondents. One black inmate, for example, had refused to speak with me until an inmate ally (himself an interviewee) agreed to participate in the interview. The prisoner subsequently described a sequence in which he was involved with an enigmatic group of "friends" who eventually served as the catalyst for delusional fear. My inmate colleague was able to place the crisis in context by linking it to predatory prison games:

Interviewer:
He said "look, I know somebody was saying something, I know that there was something going on in fact," and then he seems to be saying that as it went along, maybe it went out of control. He wasn't exactly saying, but he was implying that maybe it was my imagination at some point as far as everybody being against me. He sees that as being a mental thing. But he seemed pretty strong on saying that whatever began that situation at the time seemed real to him. Like he definitely heard people—because he said for the first two weeks that people were around him, and then they separated from him.

Inmate collaborator: Right.

Interviewer:
I wonder if those are the friends he's talking about.

Inmate collaborator:
I just was feeling the same thing—since you pointed it up I've been thinking about it. Like it happens, in Riker's Island, when a new guy comes in, they put him through the third degree. They shoot you down, and see what's happening from you, where you come from, where you're at. How much time you're doing, what you got busted for, this and that, you know? And then they start—one of the group will stay there while the others fade back, you understand, and find out more about this person. And when he gets this information he shoots it back to his friends. Now if it is sex, these friends are going to say "man, we got a fag, we got a homo, shit, I'm going to get some of that, we're going to get some big ass," and all that kind of shit. So they'll start with bribing with certain things, like give him cookies and stuff. And then when they find out this don't work—this may be where his so-called friends come from. Since this don't work, you understand, they start harassing him. By calling his name, by not calling his name, by saying things to let him know they listening, they know something, you know? Say "you know the guy on 336, or something like that, he's an uptight brother," or something like that.

The generally high level of cooperation received from inmates may have been encouraged by painstaking efforts to describe affiliation with a university and independence from the prison administration. The prescriptions for rapport building described by Newman and Giallombardo were heeded; neutral interview sites were selected (when possible), and open fraternization with prison personnel was avoided.[13] These strategies may have resulted in relatively open communication. Primarily, however, the interview "sold itself," because a focus on the person's perception of his crisis departed from the impersonal enquiries about such matters routinely conducted by custodial and treatment personnel and offered the prisoner a chance to explore thoughts, feelings and problems in a supportive context.

Information gathered under conditions of high participation and involvement—like those sought in the crisis interview—is likely to be more honest and complete.[14] Requests for step by step reconstructions of crisis "in vivo" may also help men remember detailed sequences of stress. Once this information is understood in terms of the respondent's frame of reference, it can be categorized and related to other variables. For interpretations to be valid statements about a man's perceptions of his world, however, the student must begin with the person's contemporaneous understanding of his behavior, and work from there.[d]

Interview Classification

The crisis interviews were transcribed and the motive(s) for the self-destructive incident(s) classified according to a content analytic scheme evolved by Toch. All but five (or 1.5 percent) of the interviews were amenable to content analysis.[e]

The typology was constructed initially by describing the motives and messages associated with self-destructive breakdowns. The aim was to categorize the data contained in the interviews in a manner that reflected the stated concerns of the subjects themselves, rather than in terms of theoretical constructs of interest to outsiders.

In its final form, the typology involves two dimensions: the content or nature of the threat, and the locus in which the problem is identified. Each of these dimensions is differentiated into three categories, forming a nine-cell table. Some of the nine types are further subdivided, yielding a total of 16 specific types or themes.

The typology is quite complex. The interested reader can find a detailed account of the development of the typology, along with interview excerpts that illustrate crisis themes, in Toch's manuscript on prison breakdowns.[15] A brief

---

[d]An emphasis on the phenomenology of behavior originates with philosopher Edmund Husserl. This orientation has proven fruitful in the study of social deviance, as well as of self-destructive conduct. See generally: E. Husserl, *Cartesian Meditations: An Introduction to Phenomenology* (The Hague: M. Nijoff, 1960); E. Schur, *Labeling Deviant Behavior* (New York: Harper & Row, Publishers, 1971); J. Douglas, *The Social Meanings of Suicide* (Princeton University Press, 1967).

[e]Three of these interviews were conducted with psychotic inmates. The interview material was uncodable because the accounts were sparse and seemingly disconnected.

overview of this classification scheme is provided in this chapter. Themes that emerge as related to cultural background are described more fully in the analysis chapter (Chapter 4).

The broad theme groups of the typology, as summarized in Table 3-1, entail three psychological dimensions—impotence, fear, and the need for support—and three types of crisis—coping (self and environment), self-assessment (self and others), and impulse management (self and self). The typology allows for feelings of impotence that are evoked by settings or treatment, mismanaged personal histories, or urges that explode out of control. Fear may be a response to settings, interpersonal situations, or suppressed, dissociated or projected urges. Support needs may surface in reaction to intolerable settings or arbitrary treatment, abandonment (real or imagined) by significant others, or feelings that are unmanageable.

Such groupings reflect three underlying assumptions of the typology: that personality can be seen on a continuum that can combine normal, neurotic, and psychotic levels of functioning; that outside, social, and interior worlds can be seen as functionally equivalent in terms of the psychological dimensions experienced; and that crises are a transactional product of environment stresses and personal susceptibilities. This classification scheme was not constructed for the purpose of exploring ethnically linked crisis themes. The assumptions of the typology are useful for tracing themes through ethnic groups, however, because the experiences of each group may cause its members to systematically display different levels of psychological functioning and to experience different types of problems. More importantly, the logic of an analysis of cultural susceptibi-

Table 3-1
Typology of Personal Breakdowns (Gross Theme Clusters)

	Type of Difficulty		
Relevant Psychological Dimension	Coping (Self and Environment)	Self-Perception (Self and Others)	Impulse Management (Self and Self)
Impotence (manifested in situations that spawn):	Helplessness and resentment	Hopelessness and self-doubt	Catharsis and self-hate
Fear (of):	Isolation	Prison pressures	Projected or subjective danger
Need for support (from):	Staff	Significant others	Mental health personnel

Source: Hans Toch, *Men in Crisis: Human Breakdowns in Prison* (Chicago: Aldine Publishing Company, 1975), p. 24. Reprinted with permission.

lities requires a taxonomy of crisis themes that allows for the interaction of a broad range of human needs and concerns with the stresses of prison.

In the expanded form of the typology used for coding and analysis, 16 crisis themes (seven related to impotence, four to fear, and five to dependency) are treated as separate and distinct. The category names of the crisis themes are added to the original schematic version of the typology in Table 3-2. The typology is presented in its entirety in Appendix C.

Classification entailed assigning each interviewee a primary theme, and (in roughly half the cases) a secondary theme(s). A single blind design was used for coding the interviews, involving the interviewer(s) and an independent rater (Toch). This procedure was adopted to retain the interviewers' first-hand impressions while requiring that these impressions be independently verified by a coder exposed solely to the written transcript of the interview. Theme coding reliability (measured on a sample of 40 interviews) was substantial: 85-90 percent for the primary theme, and 75-80 percent for the secondary themes. All differences were negotiated, and a final code selected for each man.

Table 3-2
Typology of Breakdowns

Relevant Psychological Dimension	Type of Crises		
	Coping (Self and Environment)	Self-Perception (Self and Others)	Impulse Management (Self and Self)
Impotence	Helplessness and resentment	Hopelessness and self-doubt	Catharsis and self-hate
	IA sanctuary search	IIA self-deactivation	IIIA self-alienation
	IB self-victimization	IIB self-sentencing	IIIB self-release
		IIC self-retaliation	
Fear	Social isolation	Fear of prison pressures	Projected or subjective danger
	IC isolation panic	IID fate avoidance	IIIC self-escape
			IIID self-preservation
Need for support	Staff	Significant others	Mental health Personnel
	ID self-classification	IIE self-linking	IIIE self-intervention
	IE aid seeking	IIF self-certification	

Note: See Appendix C for an expanded version of the typology.

Assessing Reliability: The Comparison Interviews

As was mentioned earlier, interviews were conducted with non-self-destructive inmates to provide a context for interpretation of findings with men who broke down in prison. The crisis interview schedule was employed, where possible, for comparison interviews. For men who had experienced specific personal crises or problems, the interview focused on the crisis or problem in precisely the same fashion as for the self-destructive incident. However, because personal problems were occasionally still being experienced, or had terminated without the clear end point represented by a personal breakdown, it was sometimes difficult to play out the sequential schedule. Where men reported no specific problems, or where they felt they had ill-defined complaints, attempts were made to impose a focus by exploring "issues in general" with which the respondent appeared concerned. These departures from the original schedule resulted in interviews that were generally not as well organized as the efforts to explore self-destructive incidents. The themes were typically less salient and sharp than those derived from the crisis interviews. Nevertheless, the typology proved sufficiently appliable to accommodate the difficulties described in all but three (two percent) of the comparison interviews.

The generalizability of the comparison interview themes may be limited by the fact that fruitful introspection may require the focus provided by a clear-cut and personally significant experience. A man who has not undergone a crisis experience may also be less interested in self-assessment, as is indicated by the substantial turndown rate (18 percent) among comparison inmates.[16] More importantly, a resolved problem may be a less discriminating index of core personal concerns than is a crisis. It is of course true that both problems and crises involve a transactional relationship between a potential "stressor" and a person's perception of it.[17] And what is a problem for one man may be of no consequence to another. But when a problem takes on crisis proportions, when a man feels overwhelmed, immobilized and defeated by the tests he encounters, he advertises his major needs and concerns, issues that to him are vital. Many confined men have families they have left behind and may find the separation from loved ones painful. Their discomfort testifies to a need for support from significant others during imprisonment. But it is when the separation from family spawns personal crises that we see the centrality of this relationship to the person's psychological survival.

On the whole, then, the picture that emerges from the comparison interviews may not be as clear as the picture afforded by the crisis interviews. These comparison interviews, however, may be a source of valuable information regarding prison problems for which prior experiences equip men (with varying degrees of effectiveness) to cope or endure. They thus may enable us to assess the generality of the themes associated with crises for men from different cultural backgrounds. Descriptions of effective modes of survival may also identify supports that can be built up to ameliorate coping breakdowns.

The comparison interviews were classified in a fashion comparable to that employed with crisis interviews. Limited resources allowed for the transcription of less than one-quarter (30) of the comparison interviews. For these interviews, classification proceeded in the exactly the same manner as was done with the crisis interviews. For the remaining (untranscribed) comparison interviews, an alternative classification method was devised. This procedure involved members of the research team listening to the interview recording and arriving at a group summary of problem sequences and (where applicable) of the coping strategies or resources described in each interview. These summaries were then treated as interview equivalents, and classified accordingly.

The content analysis results were used to help organize our interview material to depict crises and problems experienced by inmates of different cultural groups. Dominant concerns were also related to background indices available in prison files. (These variables are described in Appendix A.) Excerpts from the interviews and comparison summaries support and illustrate our observations.

Notes

1. "Characteristics of Inmates Under Custody," published by the Department of Correctional Services, State of New York, 1972.

2. "Statistical Tables," published by the Department of Correction, City of New York, 1972.

3. Hans Toch, *Men in Crisis: Human Breakdowns in Prison* (Chicago: Aldine Publishing Compnay, 1975), p. 127.

4. Toch, *Men in Crisis*, p. 283.

5. See, for example: L. Rogler and A. Hollingshead, *Trapped: Families and Schizophrenia* (New York: John Wiley & Sons, Inc., 1965).

6. Daniel Lockwood, "Protection Survey" (unpublished manuscript, 1975); R. Johnson, "Paraprofessional and Informal Helping Networks in Correctional Settings" (unpublished manuscript, 1975).

7. Toch, *Men in Crisis*, p. 23–24.

8. H. Toch, *Violent Men: An Inquiry into the Psychology of Violence* (Chicago: Aldine Publishing Compnay, 1969).

9. R. Merton and P. Kendall, "The Focused Interview," in P. Lazarsfeld and M. Rosenbert (Eds.), *The Language of Social Research* (New York: The Free Press, 1955), pp. 476–491.

10. Toch, *Men in Crisis*.

11. Toch, *Violent Men;* W. Bennis, K. Benne, and R. Chin, *The Planning of Change* (New York: Holt, Rinehart and Winston, Inc., 1969).

12. G. Sykes, *The Society of Captives* (New York: Atheneum, 1966); Toch, *Men in Crisis.*

13. D. Newman, "Research Interviewing in Prison," *Journal of Criminal Law, Criminology and Police Science,* 49, no. 1 (July-August 1959), pp. 127–132; R. Giallombardo, "Interviewing in the Prison Community," *The Journal of Criminal Law, Criminology and Police Science,* 57, no. 3 (1966), pp. 318–324.

14. Bennis, Benne, and Chin, *Planning Change.*

15. Toch, *Men In Crisis.*

16. H. Toch, and H. Cantril, "A Preliminary Inquiry into the Learning of Values," *The Journal of Educational Psychology,* 48, no. 3 (1957), pp. 145–156; Merton and Kendall, "Focused Interview."

17. R. Lazarus, *Psychological Stress and the Coping Process* (New York: McGraw-Hill, Inc., 1966).

4

Parameters of Crisis

Who are the victims of prison crisis, and to what pressures do they succumb? Both sides of this question are explored as they relate to ethnicity. We first determine the composition of groups at risk, identifying men whose social experiences prove differentially relevant to prison. Statistics on interview theme prevalence are then used to identify the concerns that underlie culturally linked survival patterns and give shape to prison breakdowns.

Prison Risk Statistics

Our statistics on risk, like those of most other studies of self-destructive conduct in confinement, indicate that Latin and white inmates are overrepresented in the self-injury group, and blacks are underrepresented among crisis-prone inmates. The relationship between ethnicity and risk of self-injury in confinement is consistent (and strong) across both prisons and jails, as is indicated in Table 4-1.

These findings on ethnic differences in susceptibility to self-destructive breakdowns in confinement deviate from some prior research in that Latin men do not appear to be as crisis prone as depicted in other studies. White inmates, on the other hand, seem considerably more vulnerable than has been the case in some other studies. As we have noted (Chapter 2), whites have typically been either proportionately represented or overrepresented among self-mutilators. The dramatic underrepresentation of black inmates among the victims of psychological breakdown in this survey is consistent with the findings of almost every published study of physically self-destructive conduct in confinement.

The crisis interview, which stressed a man's confinement experiences over time, provides a second measure of risk, that of chronicity of breakdowns over current and past periods of incarceration. Self-destructive incidents that went unrecorded are also sometimes mentioned in the interview. When risk is viewed from the vantage point of frequency of breakdown, Latin inmates appear more vulnerable to the stresses of confinement than their black or white counterparts (see Table 4-2). This finding makes our statistics on the relative susceptibility of Latin men to the pressures of confinement more compatible with prior research.

There may, of course, be other variables associated with susceptibility to self-injury confinement. It is possible that these variables might account for the apparent difference in ethnic susceptibility?

For both the jail and prison samples, analyses were made of differential

41

Table 4-1

Relative Prevalence of Latin, Black, and White Inmates in the Crisis Groups and Confinement Populations

		Prison Risk Groups			
Ethnic Group	Crisis Group (%)	Population (%)	Chi^{2a}	Contingency Coefficient	Probability of Occurrence
Latin	22.3	13.5	8.77	0.11	0.010
Black	23.7	58.0	84.62	0.33	0.001
White	53.9	28.3	47.06	0.25	0.001
Totals	99.9 (354)	99.8 (9,555)	86.88	0.33	0.001
		Jail Risk Groups			
Ethnic Group	Crisis Group (%)	Population[b] Estimate (%)	Chi^{2a}	Contingency Coefficient	Probability of Occurrence
Latin	34.6	24.9	6.64	0.10	0.010
Black	35.2	59.1	35.03	0.23	0.001
White	30.2	16.0	16.99	0.16	0.001
Totals	100.0 (315)	100.0 (1,583)	37.68	0.24	0.001

[a]Population figures or population estimates are used to estimate the expected distribution of dependent variables in all computations that involve comparisons between the self-injury groups and confinement populations. Thus, all statistics accompanying tables that depict the relative distribution of variables in the self-injury and confinement populations are derived from tabulations that use the N of the self-injury groups as the base. This procedure was undertaken to insure that the large size of the comparison populations would not result in misleading statistical findings.

The statistics on each separate ethnic group presented in this table were derived by running each group against both remaining groups combined. Thus, this analysis entailed cross-tabulating Latins vs. non-Latins, whites vs. nonwhites, and blacks vs. nonblacks.

[b]As noted in Appendix A, official population data is available on some variables in the prisons surveyed. Population figures displayed in tables are derived from official correctional sources. For variables on which official figures are not kept in the prison, the prison comparison sample (see Chapter 3) is used to estimate population parameters. Since no comparable population figures are available for the jails surveyed, population estimates for the jails are derived from the jail comparison sample. (This sample is also described in Chapter 3.)

risk rates for the 17 available background variables to explore this possibility. Since some of these variables were dichotomized in several ways (see Appendix A), over 50 comparisons were made. Out of these comparisons, 16 reached significance at the .05 level or lower. However, for only two variables (four comparisons) do we find a significant relationship, consistent in direction, for both jails and prisons. These variables are offense and educational achievement. As can be seen in Table 4-3, an offense of personal violence or a grammar school education is associated with risk in prisons and jails, although the relationships are not as strong as that for cultural background.

Table 4–2
Relative Prevalence of Single vs. Multiple Self-destructive Breakdowns among Latin, Black, and White Crisis Interviewees

Ethnic Group	Single Incident (%)	(N)	Multiple Incidents (%)	(N)	Totals (%)	(N)
Latin	49.3	(36)	50.7	(37)	100.0	(73)
Black	62.2	(46)	37.8	(28)	100.0	(74)
White	63.5	(113)	36.5	(65)	100.0	(178)
					100.0	(325)

Note: $Chi^2 = 4.52$.
Probability of occurrence = 0.10.
Phi = 0.12.

The six remaining variables that show a relationship to risk of self-injury are: age, marital status, drug addiction, arrest history, prior penal confinement, and offense history. These variables, however, are inconsistently related to rate of crisis. Thus, findings with respect to age, marital status and addiction, which are presented in Table 4–4, indicate that the relationship between these personal characteristics and risk vary dramatically across confinement settings: whereas adolescent, single and nonaddicted inmates represent crisis-prone groups in prison, the reverse is true in jail. The same reversal occurs when criminal justice variables are considered; while first offenders and men who have never done "state time" are crisis prone in prison, experience of arrest and prior confinement is associated with self-destructive breakdowns in jail. Similarly, a history of drug-related crimes is related to survival in prison and to nonsurvival in jail (see Table 4–5).

Thus cultural background, unlike most indices of social experience, is associated with risk factors that operate equivalently across confinement settings. This remains largely the case when controls are introduced for the two other variables (educational achievement and offense), which are also consistently related to risk in prisons and jails. As can be seen in Tables 4-6 and 4-7, the introduction of educational level as a control does not alter the general relationship between ethnicity and risk. These tables show that for both levels of education the general ethnic pattern of risk persists: whites have the highest risk of crisis and blacks have the lowest risk. An additional observation is that grade school educated whites in prison have the highest risk of all categories, and black and Latin prison inmates with high school education are more crisis prone than their less formally educated counterparts.

The use of offense type as a control variable similarly does not alter the general ethnic pattern (see Table 4-8). For both violent and nonviolent offenders, prison whites show the highest risk of breakdown and blacks show the

Table 4–3
Relative Prevalence of Selected Offense and Educational Characteristics in the Crisis Groups and Confinement Populations

Offense	Prison Risk Groups		Jail Risk Groups	
	Crisis Group (%)	Population (%)	Crisis Group (%)	Population Estimate (%)
Violent offense	34.8	28.3	19.0	8.4
Nonviolent offense	65.2	71.2	81.0	91.6
Totals	100.0 (336)	100.0 (9,597)	100.0 (294)	100.0 (1,553)
	$Chi^2 = 3.01$. Probability of occurrence = 0.075. Phi = 0.07.		$Chi^2 = 13.19$. Probability of occurrence = 0.001. Phi = 0.15.	

Educational Achievement	Crisis Group (%)	Population Estimate (%)	Crisis Group (%)	Population Estimate (%)
Grammar school (or less)	51.4	25.3	40.2	30.1
High school (or better)	48.6	74.7	59.8	69.9
Totals	100.0 (313)	100.0 (610)	100.0 (286)	100.0 (1,611)
	$Chi^2 = 44.11$. Probability of occurrence = 0.001. Phi = 0.27.		$Chi^2 = 5.97$. Probability of occurrence = 0.05. Phi = 0.10.	

Table 4-4
Relative Prevalence of Selected Background Characteristics in the Crisis Groups and Confinement Populations

	Prison Risk Group		Jail Risk Group	
Age	Crisis Group (%)	Population Estimate (%)	Crisis Group (%)	Population Estimate (%)
Adolescent (under 21)	39.3	22.2	51.3	59.5
Adult (over 21)	60.7	77.8	48.7	40.5
Totals	100.0 (341)	100.0 (610)	100.0 (382)	100.0 (1,654)

Prison Risk Group: $\text{Chi}^2 = 22.61$. Probability of occurrence = 0.001. Phi = 0.18.

Jail Risk Group: $\text{Chi}^2 = 4.86$. Probability of occurrence = 0.05. Phi = 0.08.

	Prison Risk Group		Jail Risk Group	
Marital Status	Crisis Group (%)	Population Estimate (%)	Crisis Group (%)	Population Estimate (%)
Married	19.5	35.2	29.7	22.1
Unmarried	80.5	64.8	70.3	77.9
Totals	100.0 (338)	100.0 (610)	100.0 (293)	100.0 (1,619)

Prison Risk Group: $\text{Chi}^2 = 20.11$. Probability of occurrence = 0.001. Phi = 0.17.

Jail Risk Group: $\text{Chi}^2 = 4.02$. Probability of occurrence = 0.05. Phi = 0.08.

Table 4-4–Continued

Heroin Addiction	Prison Risk Group		Jail Risk Group	
	Crisis Group (%)	Population Estimate (%)	Crisis Group (%)	Population Estimate (%)
Present	23.9	48.6	52.8	40.3
Absent	76.1	51.4	47.2	59.7
Totals	100.0 (310)	100.0 (605)	100.0 (301)	100.0 (1,629)

Chi^2 = 39.96.
Probability of occurrence = 0.001.
Phi = 0.25.

Chi^2 = 8.99.
Probability of occurrence = 0.01.
Phi = 0.12.

Table 4–5
Relative Prevalence of Selected Criminal Experience Categories in the Crisis Groups and Confinement Populations

	Prison Risk Group		Jail Risk Group	
Arrest History	*Crisis Group (%)*	*Population Estimate (%)*	*Crisis Group (%)*	*Population Estimate (%)*
Present	91.5	99.4	86.3	78.8
Absent	8.5	.6	13.7	21.2
Totals	100.0 (295)	100.0 (506)	100.0 (182)	100.0 (1,063)
	Chi² = 19.34. Probability of occurrence = 0.001. Phi = 0.18.		Chi² = 3.18. Probability of occurrence = 0.075. Phi = 0.09.	
Prior Prison Experience	*Crisis Group (%)*	*Population Estimate (%)*	*Crisis Group (%)*	*Population Estimate (%)*
Present	33.2	46.2	37.4	22.4
Absent	66.8	53.8	62.6	77.6
Totals	100.0 (295)	100.0 (503)	100.0 (179)	100.0 (1,061)
	Chi² = 9.84. Probability of occurrence = 0.01. Phi = 0.13.		Chi² = 8.94. Probability of occurrence = 0.01. Phi = 0.16.	

48

Table 4-5—Continued

History of Addiction Related Crime(s)	Prison Risk Group		Jail Risk Group	
	Crisis Group (%)	Population Estimate (%)	Crisis Group (%)	Population Estimate (%)
Present	19.3	44.9	54.4	39.7
Absent	80.7	55.1	45.6	60.3
Totals	100.0 (295)	100.0 (506)	100.0 (182)	100.0 (1,063)

Prison Risk Group: $Chi^2 = 43.11$. Probability of occurrence = 0.001. Phi = 0.27.

Jail Risk Group: $Chi^2 = 7.31$. Probability of occurrence = 0.01. Phi = 0.14.

Table 4-6
Relative Prevalence of Latin, Black, and White Inmates in the Prison Crisis Group and Population: Controlling for Educational Achievement

	Latin (%)	Black (%)	White (%)	Totals (%)
		Crisis Group		
High school education	8.4	14.5	25.7	48.6 (151)
Grade school education	13.8	8.7	28.9	51.4 (160)
Totals	22.2	23.2	54.6	100.0 (311)
		Prison Population (Estimates)		
	Latin (%)	Black (%)	White (%)	Totals (%)
High school education	8.0	50.7	15.9	74.6
Grade school education	4.9	12.3	8.2	25.4
Totals	12.9	63.0	24.1	100.0 (611)
		Crisis Group: Prison Population Ratio		
	Latin	Black	White	
High school education	1.59	0.44	1.74	
Grade school education	1.39	0.35	2.50	
Totals	2.98	0.79	4.24	

Table 4-7
Relative Prevalence of Latin, Black, and White Inmates in the Jail Crisis Group and Population: Controlling for Educational Achievement

	Latin (%)	Black (%)	White (%)	Totals (%)
		Crisis Group		
Grade school education	18.4	10.3	11.7	40.4 (114)
High school education	16.0	25.9	17.7	59.6 (168)
Totals	34.4	36.2	29.4	100.0 (282)
		Jail Population (Estimates)		
	Latin (%)	Black (%)	White (%)	Totals (%)
Grade school education	11.2	14.1	5.1	30.4 (469)
High school education	13.6	45.1	10.8	69.5 (1,072)
Totals	24.8	59.1	15.9	99.9 (1,541)
		Crisis Group: Jail Population Ratio		
	Latin	Black	White	
Grade school education	1.24	0.55	1.71	
High school education	1.37	0.67	1.91	
Totals	2.61	1.22	3.62	

lowest. A secondary finding is that nonviolent white offenders show a higher risk than other whites, while among Latins and blacks the violent offender has the greater risk.

The only condition under which the relationship between cultural background and risk of breakdown does not obtain occurs among violent offenders in jail. As can be seen in Table 4–9, there is an interaction between violent criminal conduct and ethnicity among jail inmates. Violent Latin inmates are not crisis prone in jail; violent black inmates are not as resilient to the stresses of detention as their nonviolent counterparts. It should be stressed that these findings may be unreliable, however, since the size of each sample is quite small. (There are only 15 Latin and 16 white violent offenders in the jail crisis sample.) In addition, violent offenders represent a minority of both comparison and crisis-prone jail inmates, accounting for less than one-fifth of each group. Thus for prison inmates, and for most jail inmates, criminal violence is not related to ethnic patterns of breakdown.

The crisis interviews allow us to spell out how ethnic susceptibilities manifest themselves in personal breakdowns. The relevance of other variables to the distribution of interview content among members of each cultural group can also be assessed.

Table 4–8

Relative Prevalence of Latin, Black, and White Inmates in the Prison Crisis Group and Population: Controlling For Offense

| | Crisis Group | | | |
	Latin (%)	Black (%)	White (%)	Total (%)
Violent offense	9.9	9.0	25.3	32.1 (114)
Nonviolent offense	13.8	14.9	39.1	67.9 (241)
Totals	22.7	23.9	64.4	100.0 (355)

| | Prison Population (Estimates) | | | |
	Latin (%)	Black (%)	White (%)	Total (%)
Violent offense	5.2	18.9	6.1	30.2 (184)
Nonviolent offense	10.0	43.4	16.4	69.8 (426)
Totals	15.2	62.3	22.5	100.0 (610)

| | Crisis Group: Prison Population Ratio | | |
	Latin	Black	White
Violent offense	1.76	0.45	2.04
Nonviolent offense	1.42	0.35	2.47
Totals	3.18	0.80	4.51

Table 4–9
Relative Prevalence of Latin, Black, and White Inmates in the Jail Crisis Group and Population: Controlling For Offense

| | Crisis Group | | | |
	Latin (%)	Black (%)	White (%)	Totals (%)
Violent offense	4.8	7.9	5.1	17.8 (56)
Nonviolent offense	29.8	27.3	25.1	82.2 (259)
Totals	34.6	35.2	30.2	100.0 (315)

| | Jail Population (Estimates) | | | |
	Latin (%)	Black (%)	White (%)	Totals (%)
Violent offense	3.0	5.0	1.9	9.9
Nonviolent offense	21.9	54.0	14.2	90.1 (1,426)
Totals	24.9	59.0	16.1	100.0 (1,582)

| | Crisis Group: Jail Population Ratio | | |
	Latin	Black	White
Violent offense	0.89	0.88	1.50
Nonviolent offense	1.49	0.55	1.94
Totals	2.38	1.43	3.44

The Ingredients of Crisis

The general shape of the concerns that spark self-destructive breakdowns among prisoners from different ethnic groups is presented in Tables 4-10 and 4-11. These tables depict the relative prevalence among Latin, black and white inmates of the psychological dimensions (Table 4-10) and crisis types (Table 4-11) included in the typology.

Table 4–10
Percentage of Each Ethnic Group Reflecting Specific Psychological Dimensions in Crisis Problem Response

| Psychological Dimensions | Ethnic Group | | |
	Latin (%) (N = 73)	Black (%) (N = 74)	White (%) (N = 178)
Impotence	60.3	59.5	66.3
Fear	30.1	74.3[a]	46.6
Support	71.2[a]	41.9	56.2

Note: Each individual interview could reflect more than one psychological dimension.

[a]Ethnic differences significant below 0.05 level. Chi square test.

Table 4-11
Percentage of Each Ethnic Group Reflecting Specific Type of
Difficulty in Crisis Problem Response

Crisis Types	Ethnic Group		
	Latin (%) (N = 73)	Black (%) (N = 74)	White (%) (N = 178)
Coping	35.6	44.6	36.0
Self-assessment	79.5	66.2	77.0
Impulse management	37.0	58.1[a]	38.2

Note: Each individual interview could reflect more than one crisis type.

[a]Ethnic differences significant below 0.05 level. Chi square test.

As can be seen in Table 4-10, an equal percentage of each ethnic group reflect the Impotence dimension (nearly two-thirds). Although the Fear dimension characterizes three-quarters of blacks (74 percent), it is found among only 30 percent of Latins and 47 percent of whites. Need for Support is found among seven out of ten Latins, but only occurs for 42 and 56 percent, respectively, of black and white prisoners. Thus Latins are high in the Support dimension, and blacks are high in the Fear dimension. In general, the white profile seems less distinctive than that of the other groups.

Analysis of the types of difficulty (crisis types) experienced by men from different cultural backgrounds reveals less salient patterns. Table 4-11 shows that the distribution of Latins and whites on the crisis types of the typology is very similar. Nearly 80 percent of each group have Self-Assessment problems, but only about 40 percent of each group have Coping or Impulse Management problems. Blacks, on the other hand, are more likely to have Impulse Management difficulties than the other two groups, and somewhat less likely to experience Self-Assessment problems than other inmates.

Ethnic differences in the specific motives and meanings associated with crisis incidents is presented in Table 4-12. This table is comprehensive and complex. Since the table summarizes a considerable amount of information, an example may help the reader to interpret the findings.

The Sanctuary Search theme (which appears at the top left-hand sector of Table 4-12) reflects an Impotence motive and falls under the Coping crisis type. The table shows that 3.7 percent of the overall interview group experience crises that embody this theme. It can also be seen that 1.4 percent of Latins, 2.7 percent of blacks, and 5.1 percent of whites have a Sanctuary Search theme.

Six of the 16 crisis themes that make up the taxonomy relate significantly to cultural background (see Table 4-12). It can be seen that the substantial representation of Latin inmates on the Support dimension and on the Self-

Table 4–12
Percentage of Self-destructive Inmates Expressing Specific Crisis Themes by Ethnic Group

Column headings: Total (N = 325) Latin (N = 73) Black (N = 74) White (N = 178)

Coping

Theme	Total (%)	Latin	Black	White
IA sanctuary search	(3.7)	1.4	2.7	5.1
IB self-victimization	(18.8)	20.5	25.7	15.2
IC isolation panic[a]	(8.9)	2.7	**20.3**	6.7
ID self-classification	(9.2)	8.2	4.1	11.8
IE aid-seeking	(4.9)	5.5	4.1	5.1

Self-Assessment

Theme	Total (%)	Latin	Black	White
IIA self-deactivation	(17.2)	11.0	16.2	20.2
IIB self-sentencing	(14.1)	16.4	9.5	15.2
IIC self-retaliation[a]	(7.1)	2.7	1.4	**11.2**
IID Fate Avoidance[a]	(24.9)	13.7	25.7	29.2
IIE self-linking[a]	(25.8)	**41.1**	23.0	20.8
IIF self-certification	(17.8)	17.8	9.5	21.3

Impulse Management

Theme	Total (%)	Latin	Black	White
IIIA self-alienation	(7.1)	9.6	6.8	6.2
IIIB self-release	(12.9)	12.3	10.8	14.0
IIIC self-escape[a]	(12.6)	5.5	**24.3**	10.7
IIID self-preservation[a]	(14.1)	11.0	**27.0**	10.1
IIIC self-intervention	(7.1)	9.6	8.1	5.6

Row groupings (left margin): Impotence (IA, IB / IIA, IIB, IIC / IIIA, IIIB); Fear (IC / IID / IIIC self-escape, IIID); Need for support (ID, IE / IIE, IIF / IIIC self-intervention).

Note: The first entry in each category in parenthesis is the percentage of total group presenting theme; the next three entries are the percentages for Latin, black, and white, respectively.

[a]Ethnic differences significant below 0.05 level. Chi square test.

Assessment type crises can be traced to breakdowns that feature a Self-Linking theme. This crisis theme is defined in the typology as "a protest against intolerable separation from significant others. . . . the person here feels that his well-being is tied to his relationship (usually with his family) and sees no satisfactory existence without such contact or link." The underrepresentation of Latin inmates on the Fear dimension stems primarily from the comparative absence of Fate Avoidance crises. Such breakdowns involve "a conclusion relating to one's inability to survive current or impending social situations (usually involving other inmates) which one fears because one sees oneself as weak, ineffective, or unable to respond."

The overrepresentation of self-destructive black inmates on the Fear dimension, as can be seen in Table 4-12, relates to the high proportion of crises that involve three of the four themes that make up this psychological dimension. The prevalence of Impulse Management crises among black inmates stems from an overrepresentation on both of the psychotic fear themes in the typology. The uniformly low proportion of dependency-related themes that characterizes suicide attempts among black convicts explains their underrepresentation on the Support dimension.

The specific fear themes that are disproportionately prevalent among suicidal black inmates include Isolation Panic, Self-Escape and Self-Preservation. Isolation Panic, as defined in the typology, is a situational coping theme that entails "a demand for release from 'panic-producing' isolation, where the person finds his confinement oppressive and fear-inspiring." Self-Escape and Self-Preservation are psychotic crisis motives that comprise a theme cluster related to "projected or subjective danger." These crisis themes reflect efforts to escape "destructive impulses which are strong and unpleasantly tension provoking," and "cumulating harm where the person builds up the conviction that he is in substantial physical danger from pervasive and all-powerful enemies."

The thematic picture for white inmates remains less discriminating than that depicted for black and Latin inmates when the distribution of crisis themes is explored (Table 4-12). The only theme that stands out for white inmates as a group—and that may account for their modest overrepresentation on the Impotence dimension and on the Self-Assessment crisis type—is that of Self-Retaliation. This theme describes crises that involve "self-punishment, where the person feels he is placed in an intolerable position as a result of his own past acts, and feels angry and resentful at himself."

In addition to applying the Chi Square Test to the three group comparisons, comparison was made of the difference between each pair of groups on the six crisis themes that emerged as linked to cultural background. This more detailed analysis led to substantially similar conclusions. The only possible exception to this observation relates to the underrepresentation of Latin inmates on the Fate Avoidance theme when compared to black inmates. As can be seen in Table 4-13, however, the measure of strength of relationship (phi) differs by only one percentage point from the measure of association reported for the statistically reliable comparison between Latin and white inmates on the Fate Avoidance theme. The failure to attain a comparable probability level for the Latin and black comparison may be a function of sample size.

The next phase of the analysis is geared to determine whether some members of a given cultural group (such as adolescents) are particularly prone to experience the crisis theme(s) associated with that group. Other themes that emerge as overrepresented among certain members of an ethnic group are also considered. The analytic procedure for each ethnic group entails cross-tabulating crisis themes against all dichotomized background variables (see Appendix A). The focus is on the relevance (or lack of same) of available background information to the distribution of interview themes. Subsequent analysis involves comparisons between the distribution of interview content among self-destructive and non-self-destructive members of each ethnic group. The chapter concludes with a summary of the statistics on cultural patterns of susceptibility to breakdown in confinement.

Latin Breakdowns Explored

The family dependence (Self-Linking) theme occurs among self-destructive Latin inmates with equivalent frequency when controls are introduced for a host of demographic and criminal history variables, as well as for frequency of self-mutilation and for the penal setting in which the event(s) took place. The centrality of this theme among crisis-prone Latin inmates is further indicated by the fact that a cross-tabulation of other interview themes with various demogrpahic and criminal career subgroupings of Latin inmates reveals that no other themes are associated with a Latin background.

The pervasiveness of family dependence crisis may reflect the fact that Latin men who break down, like their non-self-destructive counterparts, are almost uniformly urban, lower class Puerto Ricans who are redundants clients of the criminal justice system.[a] We have noted (in Chapter 2) that the issue of family has been described by a number or researchers as a salient concern of many lower class Latin men, independent of a variety of background characteristics.

The only variable of those available in institutional files that is mildly (though nonsignificantly) related to the prevalence of family-related crises among Latin inmates is drug addiction. As can be seen in Table 4-14, Latin heroin addicts appear somewhat more likely than other Latin inmates to experience crises that feature a Self-Linking motive, while there is no such trend for black

[a]Over 90 percent of these men come from New York City. Nine out of ten have prior arrest records, and close to half have been previously incarcerated as sentenced jail or prison inmates. Seventy-five percent of self-destructive Latin prisoners were unemployed at the time of their arrest, or were employed in low-skilled laboring or service jobs.

Table 4–13

Comparison of Latins with Blacks and Whites on the Distribution of Fate Avoidance Crises

Fate Avoidance Crises	Latins vs Blacks (N = 147)				
	Latins (%)	Blacks (%)	Chi²	Phi	Probability of Occurrence
Present	13.7	25.7	2.615	0.15	0.105
Absent	86.3	74.3			
Totals	100.0 (73)	100.0 (74)			

Fate Avoidance Crises	Latins vs. Whites (N = 251)				
	Latins (%)	Blacks (%)	Chi²	Phi	Probability of Occurrence
Present	13.7	29.2	5.89	0.16	0.015
Absent	86.3	70.8			
Totals	100.0 (73)	100.0 (178)			

or white inmates. Controlling for addiction, we find that a small group of Latin addicts with a history of incarceration in jails as sentenced prisoners are disproportionately prone to Self-Linking crises. This does not hold true for comparable groups of black or white addicts (see Table 4-15).

The relative prevalence of the situational fear (Fate Avoidance) theme among suicidal Latin inmates also appears to be largely unrelated to other variables. Most crisis-prone Latin convicts, in other words, do not find peer pressure a catalyst for breakdown. There is, however, a suggestion in the data that Fate Avoidance dilemmas may be a relatively salient concern of nonviolent offenders. The size of the sample in these tabulations makes our findings highly tentative, and the results are not statistically significant. But comparisons with black and white inmates on violent offense in relationship to the Fate Avoidance theme indicates that the trend toward overrepresentation of nonviolent offenders on this theme may be unique to self-destructive Latin inmates (see Table 4-16).

Black Breakdowns Explored

The relative prevalence of fear themes among crisis-prone blacks remains unchanged when most available background indices are held constant. This finding may be partially accounted for by the fact that all but one of the black inmates in the crisis sample are urban ghetto residents (primarily from New York City). Most of these men have had extensive prior involvments with the criminal justice system.[b] Homogeneous background experiences may also explain why no other themes emerge as differentially related to black cultural experiences when controls for a variety of background factors are introduced.

We have noted that black men who injure themselves in confinement are unrepresentative of black prisoners, since ghetto blacks seem resilient to the stresses of prison. However, ghetto experiences, as we observed in Chapter 2, can sometimes breed an exaggerated concern for personal safety. Within the atypical group of black inmates for whom ghetto socialization does not provide insulation from prison threats, some men seem more prone than others to experience crises of fear.

The Isolation Panic theme, for example, is disproportionately prevalent among younger black inmates. This theme characterizes the crises of close to half of the black adolescents in the interview sample. By contrast, only one out of ten black adult interviewees succumb to such pressures (see Table 4-17). Controlling for age, we find that 83 percent (5/6) of black adolescent violent offenders experience Isolation Panic crises, compared with 32 percent (6/19) of their nonviolent counterparts (chi^2 = 3.08; phi = 0.44; probability = .08). The

---

[b]Ninety-three percent of self-destructive black prisoners had prior arrest records; 40 percent had served at least one prior prison or jail term. Eight out of ten of these men were unemployed or sporadically employed in low-status jobs prior to confinement.

Table 4-14
Relative Prevalence of Self-linking Crises among Addict and Nonaddict Members of Each Ethnic Group

Latin: Addiction (N = 51)

Self-linking Crises	Present (%)	Absent (%)	Chi^2	Phi	Probability of Occurrence
Present	59.1	34.5	2.15	0.24	0.14
Absent	40.9	65.5			
Totals	100.0 (21)	100.0 (29)			

Black: Addiction (N = 63)

Self-linking Crises	Present (%)	Absent (%)	Chi^2	Phi	Probability of Occurrence
Present	21.4	22.9	0.03	0.02	0.86
Absent	78.6	77.1			
Totals	100.0 (28)	100.0 (35)			

Table 4-4—Continued

| Self-linking Crises | White: Addiction (N = 151) | | Chi² | Phi | Probability of Occurrence |
	Present (%)	Absent (%)			
Present	27.3	18.6	0.71	0.09	0.40
Absent	72.7	81.4			
Totals	100.0 (42)	100.0 (118)			

Table 4–15
Relative Prevalence of Self-linking Crises among Latin, Black, and White Addicts by Jail Sentences Served

Self-linking Crises	*Latins: Prior Jail Term (N = 17)*		*Fischer's Exact Test*
	Present (%)	*Absent (%)*	
Present	80.0	28.6	
			0.05
Absent	20.0	71.4	
Totals	100.0 (10)	100.0 (7)	
Self-linking Crises	*Blacks: Prior Jail Term (N = 22)*		*Fischer's Exact Test*
	Present (%)	*Absent (%)*	
Present	11.1	30.8	
			0.57
Absent	88.9	69.2	
Totals	100.0 (9)	100.0 (13)	
Self-linking Crises	*Whites: Prior Jail Term (N = 26)*		*Fischer's Exact Test*
	Present (%)	*Absent (%)*	
Present	21.4	25.0	
			0.80
Absent	78.6	75.0	
Totals	100.0 (14)	100.0 (12)	

relationship among age, and among age, offense, and the Isolation Panic theme does not obtain for Latin or white inmates, or emerges there in highly diluted form (see Table 4-18).

The only background factor related to the prevalence of psychotic fear themes among black inmates is that of the penal settings in which the self-destructive incident(s) occurred. Their Self-Preservation crisis are considerably more likely to occur in prison than in jail. Confinement setting does not play an equivalent role in the Self-Preservation breakdowns of Latin or white inmates (see Table 4-19).

White Breakdowns Explored

We have seen that the only theme that differentiates white inmates as a group from Latin and black convicts is that of guilt-induced Self-Retaliation. This crisis

Table 4-16

Relative Prevalence of Fate Avoidance Crises among Latin, Black, and White Inmates by Violent Offense

| Fate Avoidance Crises | Latins: Current Violent Offense (N = 57) | | | | |
	Present (%)	Absent (%)	Chi^2	Phi	Probability of Occurrence
Present	4.0	21.9	2.38	0.25	0.12
Absent	96.0	78.1			
Totals	100.0 (25)	100.0 (32)			

| Fate Avoidance Crises | Blacks: Current Violent Offense (N = 67) | | | | |
	Present (%)	Absent (%)	Chi^2	Phi	Probability of Occurrence
Present	17.4	31.8	0.95	0.15	0.33
Absent	82.6	68.2			
Totals	100.0 (23)	100.0 (44)			

Table 4-16—Continued

| | Whites: Current Violent Offense (N = 160) | | | |
Fate Avoidance Crises	Present (%)	Absent (%)	Chi²	Phi	Probability of Occurrence
Present	26.3	29.5	0.03	0.03	0.86
Absent	73.7	70.5			
Totals	100.0 (38)	100.0 (122)			

Table 4–17
Relative Prevalence of Isolation Panic Crises among Black Inmates by Age

Isolation Panic	Age (N = 72)		Chi^2	Phi	Probability of Occurrence
	Adolescent (%)	Adult (%)			
Present	44.0	8.5	10.4	0.42	0.001
Absent	56.0	91.5			
Totals	100.0 (25)	100.0 (47)			

Table 4–18
Relative Prevalence of Isolation Panic Crises among Latin and White Inmates by Age and Age in Conjunction with Offense

Isolation Panic	Adolescent (%)	*Latins: Age (N = 69)* Adult (%)	Chi²	Phi	Probability of Occurrence
Present	6.9	0.0			
			0.92	0.20	0.34
Absent	93.1	100.0			
Totals	100.0 (29)	100.0 (40)			

Isolation Panic	Adolescent (%)	*Whites: Age (N = 164)* Adult (%)	Chi²	Phi	Probability of Occurrence
Present	9.2	2.6			
			2.12	0.14	0.15
Absent	90.8	97.4			
Totals	100.0 (87)	100.0 (77)			

Table 4-18—Continued

Latins: Age/Offense (N = 29)

Isolation Panic	Adolescent: Violent Offense (%)	Adolescent: Nonviolent Offense (%)	Chi²	Phi	Probability of Occurrence
Present	16.7	4.3			
			0.02	0.20	0.88
Absent	83.3	95.6			
Totals	100.0 (6)	99.9 (23)			

Whites: Age/Offense (N = 87)

Isolation Panic	Adolescent: Violent Offense (%)	Adolescent: Nonviolent Offense (%)	Chi²	Phi	Probability of Occurrence
Present	9.1	9.2			
			0.30	0.001	0.59
Absent	90.9	90.8			
Totals	100.0 (11)	100.0 (76)			

Table 4-19

Relative Prevalence of Self-preservative Crises among Black, Latin, and White Inmates by Setting of Crisis

Self-preservation Crises	Blacks: Confinement Setting (N = 66)				
	Prison (%)	Jail (%)	Chi^2	Phi	Probability of Occurrence
Present	45.2	14.3			
			6.21	0.34	0.01
Absent	54.8	85.7			
Totals	100.0 (31)	100.0 (35)			

Self-preservation Crises	Latins: Confinement Setting (N = 65)				
	Prison (%)	Jail (%)	Chi^2	Phi	Probability of Occurrence
Present	14.3	9.1			
			0.04	0.08	0.84
Absent	85.7	90.9			
Totals	100.0 (21)	100.0 (44)			

Table 4-19—Continued

	Whites: Confinement Setting (N = 159)				
Self-preservation Crises	*Prison (%)*	*Jail (%)*	*Chi²*	*Phi*	*Probability of Occurrence*
Present	7.2	13.2	0.95	0.10	0.33
Absent	92.8	86.8			
Totals	100.0 (83)	100.0 (76)			

theme relates to only a minority (11 percent) of white interviewees. The absence of a prominent theme(s) when white inmates are treated as a homogeneous category is a result that was anticipated (see Chapter 2) when we considered the diverse groups that might plausibly fall under the social rubric "white male," and even "lower class white male." Relevant social experience groups may be defined in terms of background factors related to theme prevalence.

Background correlates are not much help with respect to the differential manifestation of Self-Retaliation crises, since only 20 men are involved and the statistical relationships are tenuous. Some clues about the connotations of this theme, however, are provided by slight (nonsignificant) associations between the Self-Retaliation theme, occupational status and prison experience. As can be seen in Table 4-20, skilled laborers and white collar workers (who may be middle class by prison standards) are somewhat more likely to experience Self-Retaliation crises. This is also the case for men who have served one or more prior prison terms. The interviews that feature a Self-Retaliation theme provide a link between these background factors and self-punishment sequences.

Two prevalent themes relate to major indices of social experience among crisis-prone white inmates: Fate Avoidance and Self-Certification. We have noted that the Fate Avoidance theme involves the feeling that one in unable to stand up to prison pressure, particularly in the form of threats posed by other inmates. Self-Certification dilemmas entail a different type of threat, that signalled by impending dissolution of important emotional ties. The aim of self-mutilation incidents with a Self-Certification motive is to "convince the other party in a degenerating or terminating relationship of one's seriousness, affect, or inability to survive." By thus resorting to an extreme declaration of need, the person hopes to refurbish his ties to significant others.

Taken together, the Fate Avoidance and Self-Certification themes characterize the breakdowns of approximatly one-half of the white interviewees. They are also somewhat more common among whites as a group than among Latin or black prisoners. These crisis motives (like the Self-Retaliation theme) fall under the Self-Assessment crisis type in the typology, a theme cluster that comprizes three out of every four self-destructive white inmates. The differential prevalence of these themes across background characteristics may thus provide a means of subdividing white inmates into groups with special susceptibilities.

The background correlates of the fear (Fate Avoidance) theme among white inmates include age and setting of crisis. Young white inmates are disproportionately prone to this type of crisis; over one-third of such men succumb to peer pressure. Fate Avoidance crises are endemic among young white inmates in jail, accounting for over half of the white adolescents who experience jail crises. When we control for age and penal setting of self-injury, young white inmates emerge as substantially more susceptible to Fate Avoidance breakdowns than their Latin and black contemporaries (Table 4-21).

69

Table 4–20
Relative Prevalence of Self-retaliation Crises among White Inmates by Occupation and Prison Experience

Self-certification Crises	Occupation (N = 93)		Chi²	Phi	Probability of Occurrence
	Low-skilled Laborers (%)	Craftsmen and Semiwhite-Collar Workers (%)			
Present	8.3	19.0	0.99	0.14	0.32
Absent	91.7	81.0			
Totals	100.0 (72)	100.0 (21)			

Self-certification Crises	Prison Experience (N = 134)		Chi²	Phi	Probability of Occurrence
	Present (%)	Absent (%)			
Present	16.2	7.2	1.55	0.135	0.21
Absent	83.8	92.8			
Totals	100.0 (37)	100.0 (97)			

Table 4–21

Relative Prevalence of Fate Avoidance Crises among Adolescents and among Adolescents with Jail Incidents by Ethnic Group

Fate Avoidance Crises	Latin (%)	Black (%)	White (%)	Chi^2	Phi	Probability of Occurrence
			Adolescents (N = 141)			
Present	17.2	28.0	39.1	4.98	0.18	0.09
Absent	82.8	72.0	60.9			
Totals	100.0 (29)	100.0 (25)	100.0 (87)			

Fate Avoidance Crises	Latin (%)	Black (%)	White (%)	Chi^2	Phi	Probability of Occurrence
		Adolescents: Jail Crisis (N = 55)				
Present	8.7	30.0	54.5	11.07	0.41	0.004
Absent	91.3	70.0	45.5			
Totals	100.0 (23)	100.0 (10)	100.0 (22)			

The primary ingredients of support (Self-Certification) crises among white prisoners are age and offense; younger white inmates are prone to use break-downs to firm up flagging relationships, as are persons (and particularly adolescents) with nonviolent criminal careers. Each of these interactions occurs only among white inmates and identifies men whose preprison experiences foster Self-Certification crises (see Table 4-22).

We have seen that the dominant concerns of crisis-prone Latin and black inmates are largely unrelated to demographic and criminal career variables. For white inmates, on the other hand, subdivision in terms of age and some criminal experience categories reveals groups with specific types of vulnerability to prison stress. We round out our statistical exploration of differential susceptibility to prison pressure by comparing the relative prevalence of problem and crisis themes for each ethnic group.

The Shape Of Prison Problems

The comparison interview sample, as was noted in Chapter 3, makes it possible to determine the representativeness of the concerns associated for each ethnic group with prison breakdown. In this section we contrast the distribution of interview themes for self-destructive and comparison inmates from each ethnic group and discuss the implications of comparative trends.

Latin Prisoners

Self-destructive Latin inmates, as can be seen in Table 4-23, do not differ from their non-self-destructive counterparts on the theme clusters of the typology. For both groups the primary psychological dimension involved in prison stress is the Need for Support, and the prominent crisis type is that of Self-Assessment.

A similar picture emerges when we consider the 16 themes that make up the typology. Table 4-24 shows that the modal prison problem of Latin inmates in general relates to family ties, with a large majority of comparison inmates citing family problems as their main cause of discomfort in prison. Notable differences between the distribution of problem and crisis themes do show up in the comparative overrepresentation of Fate Avoidance themes among a random sample of Latin men, and the relative overrepresentation of dependency bids to staff (Aid Seeking and Self-Intervention crises) among self-destructive Latin prisoners. These latter (support) themes involve staff in ameliorative roles. In Aid Seeking crises, staff are called upon to resolve physical problems, usually by providing medication. In Self-Intervention crises, prison personnel are requested to provide professional mental health assistance in the management of feelings and moods. Although the themes of Self-Certification and Self-Preservation are

Table 4-22
Relative Prevalence of Self-certification Crises among Adolescents, Nonviolent Criminals, and Nonviolent Adolescent Criminals by Ethnic Group

Self-certification Crises	Latin (%)	Black (%)	White (%)	Chi^2	Phi	Probability of Occurrence
	Adolescents (N = 141)					
Present	20.7	4.0	31.0	8.07	0.23	0.02
Absent	79.3	96.0	69.0			
Totals	100.0 (29)	100.0 (25)	100.0 (87)			
	Nonviolent Criminal Career Cases (N = 85)					
Self-certification Crises	Latin (%)	Black (%)	White (%)	Chi^2	Phi	Probability of Occurrence
Present	9.1	0.0	31.1	7.24	0.28	0.03
Absent	90.9	100.0	68.9			
Totals	100.0 (11)	100.0 (13)	100.0 (61)			

Table 4-22—Continued

Self-certification Crises	Adolescent: Nonviolent Criminal Career Cases (N = 59)					
	Latin (%)	Black (%)	White (%)	Chi^2	Phi	Probability of Occurrence
Present	0.0	0.0	35.4			
				5.47	0.29	0.06
Absent	100.0	100.0	64.6			
Totals	100.0 (3)	100.0 (8)	100.0 (48)			

Table 4-23

Percentage of Crisis Prone and Comparison Latin Inmates Reflecting Specific Psychological Dimensions and Types of Difficulty in Crisis Problem Response

Psychological Dimensions	Sample	
	Latin Crisis Group (%) (N = 73)	Latin Comparison Group (%) (N = 48)
Impotence	60.3	66.6
Fear	30.1	33.3
Support	71.2	75.0

Crisis Types	Sample	
	Latin Crisis Group (%) (N = 73)	Latin Comparison Group (%) (N = 48)
Coping	35.6	39.6
Self-assessment	79.5	87.5
Impulse management	37.0	33.3

Note: Each individual interview could reflect more than one psychological dimension or crisis type.

also more common among crisis-prone Latins than comparisons, these themes are particularly prevalent among adolescent whites and prison blacks, respectively. They are therefore discussed in chapters that explore the susceptibilities of these men.

Black Prisoners

The concerns of the few black men who injure themselves in confinement differ radically from those of a more representative sample of black prisoners. As can be seen in Table 4-25, relatively few black comparison interviewees experience problems that relate to the Fear dimension or the Impulse Management crisis type in the typology. Such men seem more likely than our marginal group of crisis-prone black convicts to encounter difficulties that reflect Impotence concerns.

Differences between self-destructive and comparison black prisoners are highlighted when the relative distribution of problem and crisis themes are compared. Table 4-26 shows that comparison inmates are underrepresented on the

Table 4–24
Percentages of Crisis Prone and Comparison Latin Inmates Expressing Specific Crisis or Problem Themes

	Coping *Total (N = 121) Latin Crisis Group (N=73) Latin Comparison Group (N = 48)*	Assessment	Impulse Management
Impotence	IA sanctuary search (4.1) 1.4 8.3 IB self-victimization (24.0) 20.5 29.2	IIA self-deactivation (9.9) 11.0 8.3 IIB self-sentencing (18.2) 16.4 20.8 IIC self-retaliation (4.1) 2.7 6.3	IIIA self-alienation (6.6) 9.6 2.1 IIIB self-release (14.9) 12.3 18.8
Fear	IC isolation panic (3.3) 2.7 4.2	IID fate avoidance[a] (19.0) 13.7 **27.1**	IIIC self-escape (5.8) 5.5 6.3 IIID self-preservation[a] (7.4) **11.0** 2.1 IIIC self-intervention[a] (5.8) 9.6 0
Need for support	ID self-classification (5.8) 8.2 2.1 IE aid-seeking[a] (3.3) **5.5** 0	IIE self-linking[a] (52.9) 41.1 70.8 IIF self-certification[a] (13.2) **17.8** 6.3	

Note: The first entry in each category in parentheses is the percentage of total group presenting theme; the next two entries are the percentages for self-destructive and nonself-destructive Latins, respectively.

[a]Differences significant below 0.10 level. Chi square test.

Table 4–25

Percentage of Crisis Prone and Comparison Black Inmates Reflecting Specific Psychological Dimensions and Types of Difficulty in Crisis Problem Response

Psychological Dimensions	Sample	
	Black Crisis Group (%) (N = 74)	Black Comparison Group (%) (N = 67)
Impotence	59.5	74.2
Fear	74.3[a]	34.8
Support	41.9	45.5
Crisis Types	Sample	
	Black Crisis Group (%) (N = 74)	Black Comparison Group (%) (N = 67)
Coping	44.6	42.4
Self-assessment	66.2	68.2
Impulse management	58.1[a]	40.9

Note: Each individual interview could reflect more than one psychological dimension or crisis type.

[a]Differences significant below 0.05 level. Chi square test.

psychotic Self-Deactivation and the Self-Alienation themes, less prevalent crisis motives. This table indicates that most black inmates, in contrast to the minority who break down, are prone to Impotence dilemmas. These problems reflect perceptions of oneself as a victim of arbitrary abuse by the criminal justice system or its agents (Self-Victimization) and difficulties in managing feelings of anger and resentment (Self-Release). The issue of family ties (Self-Linking) is also a somewhat more prevalent concern of black comparison inmates.

White Prisoners

The relative distribution of psychological dimensions and crisis types among self-destructive and comparison white inmates is presented in Table 4–27. This table indicates that Support themes are relatively more prevalent among the random sample of white inmates. Fear themes, on the other hand, seem comparatively rare among a representative sample of white prisoners, while there is a slight overrepresentation of Impulse Management themes among crisis cases. Neither of

Table 4–26

Percentages of Crisis Prone and Comparison Black Inmates Expressing Specific Crisis or Problem Themes

	Total (N = 141) Black Crisis Group (N = 74) Black Comparison Group (N = 67)		
	Coping	*Assessment*	*Impulse Management*
Impotence	IA sanctuary search (3.5) 2.7 4.5	IIA self-deactivation[a] (10.6) **16.2** 4.5	IIIA self-alienation[a] (3.5) **6.8** 0
	IB self-victimization[a] (33.3) 25.7 **41.8**	IIB self-sentencing (12.1) 9.5 14.9	IIIB self-release[a] (21.3) 10.8 **32.8**
		IIC self-retaliation (2.1) 1.4 3.0	
Fear	IC isolation panic[a] (10.6) **20.3** 0	IID fate avoidance (26.2) 25.7 26.9	IIIC self-escape[a] (15.6) **24.3** 6.0
			IIID self-preservation[a] (17.7) **27.0** 7.6
Need for support	ID self-classification (2.8) 4.1 1.5	IIE self-linking[a] (29.1) 23.0 **35.8**	IIIE self-intervention (5.7) 8.1 3.0
	IE aid-seeking (5.0) 4.1 6.1	IIF self-certification (6.4) 9.5 3.0	

Note: The first entry in each category in parentheses is the percentage of total group presenting theme; the next two entries are the percentages for self-destructive and nonself-destructive blacks, respectively.

[a]Differences significant below 0.10 level. Chi square test.

these latter findings, however, approaches statistical significance. The most salient feature of Table 4–27 relates to the consistently high proportion of self-destructive and non-self-destructible white inmates on the Impotence dimension. Although there is a trend toward overrepresentation of comparison interviewees on the Self-Assessment crisis type, Self-Assessment dilemmas are also prevalent among crisis-prone men. We have noted that these theme clusters relating to Impotence and Self-Assessment include distinctive crisis themes of some white inmates.

The similarities between crisis-prone and comparison white prisoners are more obvious when we compare the distributions of problem and crisis themes. As is shown in Table 4–28, the family dependence (Self-Linking) theme is the only theme that differentiates white comparison inmates from those who break down. Every other white comparison interviewee experiences family-related problems in prison, while only one-fifth of the crisis sample link prison stress to their family ties. More relevant to our exploration of white patterns of breakdown is the fact that crisis themes differentially associated with some white cultural experiences (Self-Retaliation, Fate Avoidance, and Self-Certification)

Table 4–27

Percentage of Crisis Prone and Comparison White Inmates Reflecting Specific Psychological Dimensions and Types of Difficulty in Crisis Problem Response

Psychological Dimensions	Sample	
	White Crisis Group (%) (N = 178)	White Comparison Group (%) (N = 31)
Impotence	66.3	64.5
Fear	46.6	32.2
Support	56.2	74.2[a]

Crisis Types	Sample	
	White Crisis Group (%) (N = 178)	White Comparison Group (%) (N = 31)
Coping	36.0	32.2
Self-assessment	77.0	90.3
Impulse management	38.2	29.3

Note: Each individual interview could reflect more than one psychological dimension or crisis type.

[a]Difference significant below 0.10 level. Chi square test.

are also a prevalent concern of comparison interviewees. The congruity between the concerns of self-destructive and comparison white inmates is further indicated by the equivalent representation of most of the Self-Assessment themes in both groups.

Summary

Latin men are disproportionatley susceptible to crises in confinement that involve threats to their family ties. Crisis-prone white inmates, who represent a substantial risk group, experience less distinctive prison problems. As a group, these men seem prone to neurotic crises of self-punishment; those who are younger or less experienced in crime, on the other hand, are susceptible to crises that relate to fear of peers and resentment over unstable personal relationships. The issue of personal safety is the most salient concern of the few black inmates who break down in confinement.

Table 4-28
Percentages of Crisis Prone and Comparison White Inmates Expressing Specific Crisis or Problem Themes

	Total (N = 209)	White Crisis Group (N = 178)	White Comparison Group (N = 31)
	Coping	*Assessment*	*Impulse Management*
Impotence	IA sanctuary search (5.3) 5.1 6.5	IIA self-deactivation (20.1) 20.2 19.4	IIIA self-alienation (5.3) 6.2 0
	IB self-victimization (16.3) 15.2 22.6	IIB self-sentencing (15.8) 15.2 19.4	IIIB self-release (14.8) 14.0 19.4
		IIC self-retaliation (12.4) 11.2 19.4	
Fear	IC isolation panic (5.7) 6.7 0	IID fate avoidance (28.2) 29.2 22.6	IIIC self-escape (9.6) 10.7 3.2
			IIID self-preservation (9.6) 10.1 6.5
Need for support	ID self-classification (11.0) 11.8 6.5	IIE self-linking[a] (24.9) 20.8 48.4	IIIE self-intervention (4.8) 5.6 0
	IE aid-seeking (4.8) 5.1 3.2	IIF self-certification (21.5) 21.3 22.6	

Note: The first entry in each category in parentheses is the percentage of total group presenting theme; the next two entries are the percentages for self-destructive and nonself-destructive whites, respectively.

[a]Differences significant below 0.10 level. Chi square test.

The comparison interview survey suggests that the family-centered crisis pattern of Latin inmates is representative of the concerns of most Latin prisoners. Similarly, the neurotic crisis themes of white inmates reflect concerns shared by many white prisoners. Crisis-prone black convicts, by contrast, stand apart from their prison peers. Ghetto socialization does not spawn fear in prison for most lower class black inmates, but rather leads to pragmatic concerns with victimization and resentment.

In the next three chapters our perspective shifts from the statistics of crisis to a more intimate look at the pressures that impinge on men who break down. Our focus is on stress as it is experienced by the man in crisis and our goal is to trace prison survival to its roots in cultural experience. We show that family-dependent Latin men find prison especially cold and lonely (Chapter 5), while traumatized ghetto blacks overreact to the threats posed in confinement (Chapter 6). For some white inmates we see that a semi-middle-class background can foster problems of guilt and self-hatred after incarceration. For others, sheltered life experiences can create susceptibility to panic in the face of peer pressure and resentment when significant others fail to ameliorate prison stress (Chapter 7).

5   Sons and Mothers

Studies employing various indices of stress have traced prevalent Latin coping difficulties to the family. The only statistically significant difference between Puerto Rican male schizophrenics and controls in one major study involved differential perception of the mother: schizophrenics tended to see their mothers as less loving and affectionate than did the controls.[1] Hysterical seizures (sometimes referred to as the Puerto Rican ataque) are a relatively common response to intrafamily stress;[2] periods of enforced separation from family (e.g., for medical hospitalization) have been associated with extreme separation anxiety.[3] The prevalence among Latin men of neurotic conflicts centered around problems of defiance and submission to authority figures has been linked to the Latin family experience.[4]

The use of suicide gestures or hysterical attacks to communicate needs may be pathological extensions of relationships and communication techniques learned in the Latin family.[5] Neurotic conflicts regarding relationships to authority figures may reflect the extremes that dependency problems fostered by Latin families can reach.[6]

Our findings, and those of other studies, indicate that Latin men are disproportionately prone to crises of self-mutilation and attempted suicide in penal settings. The uniquely prevalent concern of Latin inmates for support from their families suggests that incarceration aggravates susceptibilities created by the Latin family experience because it separates the Latin prisoner from his primary source of support.[7] Thus many Latin convicts find that signs of love and concern are least available when they are most strongly needed. The separation from family may be stressful for most Latin inmates; for the more dependent and family-centered Latin inmates, the experience may prove unmanageable.

This chapter is divided into three sections devoted, respectively, to the stress of family support loss, to problems associated with excessive family attachments, and to handicaps that derive from family-related expectations about prison life. We see that most Latins experience difficulties in one or more of these areas; for some prisoners, these issues are linked to psychological survival.

Separation and Anxiety

Fully seven out of ten randomly selected Puerto Rican inmates experienced—and assimilated—stress in confinement that was related to their family ties (see

81

Chapter 4). These men speak primarily of the pain and emptiness that accompanies separation from family, and express concern for loved ones whose lives may be adversely affected by their incarceration. The problems of typical interviewees were summarized[a] as follows:

ATT Comparison 16:

There is the problem of being separated from people to whom he feels really close. Although he has heterosexual attachments, he talks about these pains really being confined to blood relatives, and there's a certain amount of loneliness. In his cell he has his mind turned to thoughts of his family and he misses them a great deal.

ARS Comparison DD:

He is an inmate whose major problem in prison is his separation from his family and this takes two forms: One is missing his mother and wishing he was with her and receiving support from her and the second is missing his baby sister, whom he feels he should be out there helping. It makes him feel bad that he's not out there to play the appropriate roles.

The problem of loneliness is a continuing one for many confined Latin men. Although the problem usually proves manageable, the fact that one is apart from people that one loves may be unpleasantly accentuated by even brief interruptions in the flow of family support, such as when an expected visit fails to materialize, or by the intrusion of painful thoughts about family that may emerge during "dead time" spent in prison cells. For example:

---

[a]To avoid confusion, it should be reiterated that it was impossible to transcribe most of the comparison interviews. Where possible, comparison interview transcripts will be used to illustrate points. For the most part, however, study group summaries (see chapter 3) are the only interview materials available to highlight comparison themes.

Abbreviations are used to denote the penal institutions in which the various interviews occurred. Abbreviations for the prisons surveyed include: ATT (Attica), AUB (Auburn), CL (Clinton), CX (Coxsackie), DSH or MSH (Prison Mental Hospitals), EAST (Eastern), EL (Elmira), GH (Green Haven), GM (Great Meadow), and SS (Sing Sing). Jail abbreviations include ARS (Adolescent Remand Shelter), MHDM (Manhattan House of Detention for Men), and RIH (Riker's Island Hospital).

Comparison interviews are indicated by the (abbreviated) name of the prison at which the interview was conducted, the sample name (comparison), and the number of the interviewee in the group of interviews conducted at a given institution. Thus, the sixteenth man interviewed in the comparison sample at Attica prison would be listed as ATT Comparison 16.

For interviewees in the crisis sample, the same designation format is used, except that no sample status is indicated. Thus, the sixteenth man in the crisis interview group at Attica prison would be listed as ATT 16.

GH Comparison 12:
> A few days a week when you start thinking about the street and your wife. . . . Maybe you're expecting a visit. Like this past week I was expecting a visit and I didn't get it. There comes a time when you feel lonely.

ARS Comparison D:
> Like I got a family out there and I would like to be with them, you know? And that keeps on going in my mind. And like if I have something to do, it won't bother me, you know? See, we lock in most of the day, and we can't be doing nothing. Mop, sweep, I don't care, just to have something to do. I'd be feeling better. . . . I try to do something but in the background there's nothing to do. The cell is so bare, you can't do nothing in it.

Some Latin men experience— and somehow weather— fairly substantial disruptions of their family supports. Deaths among relatives or abandonment by family, for example, are traumas which impinged strongly on some Latin convicts, spawning depression, thoughts of suicide, or resignation to a life that seems devoid of meaningful rewards. There is also a minority of comparison inmates whose crises were still in progress and who described sequences that may contain the seeds of breakdown. Such men see their fate as tied to their relationships with significant others (usually wives or mothers) and experience episodes in which they are racked by doubts about the reliability of their family supports. As is illustrated in the following interview summary, the line that separates such men from the inmates who overtly break down can be exceedingly slim:

EAST Comparison 9:
> He mentions that at times he can doubt the commitment of his wife for no reason at all and at other times he says he's tied to such cues as delayed mail or relatively infrequent visits or even ambiguous mail, which can trigger uncertainty about his wife's attachment to him. . . . And when he considers the possibility of being abandoned by his wife, he fantasizes, however briefly, fairly concrete suicidal thoughts, including tying ropes around cell bars, tying his hands behind his back and then standing on a stool and kicking free from the stool. Although he goes out of his way to communicate to me that this is not a firm resolution on his part, it seems clear that this is something that he's tossing over in his mind and it seems to be contingent on what the decision about his family ties will be.

The pains of separation from family remain manageable for Latin inmates who do not depend on family support alone to weather the stresses of prison. These men may find their supports are strained, but not broken, by incarceration; they feel lonely because they are apart from loved ones, but they do not feel completely abandoned; their lives are less satisfying, but they do not lack meaning or purpose. To cope, they avail themselves of surrogate supports in prison that help them deemphasize their emotional involvements with their families and thus avert crises of loneliness or abandonment.

Inmates with dependency problems, for example, attest to the supportive role played by concerned cellmates, who can provide assistance by maintaining a tactful silence about family matters, or by imparting a sense of perspective on such problems:

ARS Comparison D:

I try to do something like write a letter or talk to my cellie, and he helps me a lot, because he's got something in his head, you know? And he talks to me. I think if I hadn't gotten (this) cellie, I had four cellies and I had to get transferred from them, because they start talking home and everything, it bugs me out. My cellie don't talk about home, because he's been here for twelve months already.

ATT Comparison 15:

The thing that saved me was my cell partner. . . . my cell partner was an old timer, he had been in jail a long time. He talked to me. And what he told me made sense. He said when you're out you'll still be a young man and that there are other women, and you know how love is. So I got over it.

Therapeutically oriented staff can also play ameliorative roles with dependent men. As is shown in the following interview summary, staff can provide help in the management of family-related problems which ranges from professional counselling to informal, on-the-spot advice and support:

GM Comparison 10:

In discussing the path out of this unpleasant period (of loneliness) he definitely does credit prison staff with aiding him substantially, both in terms of his relationship with therapeutic staff (he apparently went to counselling interviews weekly and received some support in the sense of advice that helped him think less about these outside), but also with respect to his encounters with guards, who he testifies went out of their way to give him useful advice and the advice they gave him when they sought him out as a new arrival was that he would be better off if he found some way not to dwell on the outside. Apparently in terms of the way he describes himself now that advice has been turned into practice and works for him.

Thus the ties that bind Latin inmates to their families are strong, but they need not represent lifelines. When confined, some men do manage with attenuated family ties, or with the absence of family support. And their depencency needs may be mild enough to allow substitute supports to reduce the pains of separation from family.

Latin inmates who injure or attempt to kill themselves, on the other hand, are traumatized by separation from significant others and seem unable to face prison without direct family contact and support. The extent of their family dependency can be substantial and suffocating. It can create problems of guilt over the harm their incarceration has done to loved ones, and resentment about their inability to achieve independence and withstand the stresses of prison. Such dependency needs can also make penal settings seem disproportionately alien and cold, and can promote crises when prison staff refuse (or are unable) to play required parental roles.

The Crisis Of Abandonment

Over 40 percent of self-destructive Puerto Rican interviewees experienced Self-Linking crises (see Chapter 4). These men, in contrast to their non-self-destructive counterparts, see their survival in confinement as a *direct corollary* of their family ties:

MHDM 20:
> See, my only hope is my wife and my kids, you know. That's what I have to live for. Otherwise I—life don't mean nothing to me.

ARS H:
> I ain't got nobody to go to but them, my mother and my family. What's the sense of me living if they don't want me: If they don't want me around, what can I do? I can't wander the world alone, so why not kill myself?

Many crisis-prone Latin men stipulate that support from significant others must be by definition forthcoming while they are confined. As one inmate put it, "a mother is a mother no matter what." In explaining suicide attempts, such men tell us they have found their family lifelines too suddenly and arbitrarily cut off after they have been incarcerated:

EL 2:
> All I wanted was someone to help me out, and that was my mother. And she turned me down ... what was the use of me keep on living without nothing to fight for, without any family? Like there was nothing left for me, nothing else to do.

ARS 4:
> My case went to Supreme Court, and my wife didn't appear, my mother didn't appear. They didn't care for me, so what's the sense of me living? ... So I came back to my cell, and I sat down and started thinking. Tears started running down my eyes. So I said "Nobody cares for me on the outside, what's the sense of me living?"

The passage of time guarantees that families will grow away from imprisoned men. Latin inmates undergoing long sentences deplore this consequence of imprisonment:

DSH 16:
My young brother was just seven years old when I first went to prison. I turn around, and he's in the army now. My younger sister was fifteen, and she's married now and has a son of her own, four years old. And right after me, I'm nothing. There's nothing really there. So before I knew it I was putting lighter fluid all over the cell, myself. And I set myself on fire.

For the more brittle and dependent men, the simple fact of separation from family can promote preoccupation with the fragility of family links. It can also affect the capacity to control feelings (Self-Release crises) because it removes the sources of personal stability:

I: When you were in here, were you thinking about your brothers and sisters and your mother and how much you missed them?

RIH 5:
Yeah, right. That's what really killed me. It hurt me, it burns me. It like burns my heart when I think about something like this, it burns my heart. And that's what makes me go explode and go crazy.

ARS H:
The only thing, when I be inside this cell eighteen hours doing nothing, and you be thinking about home, you think about what's happening, or somebody come up to visit you and say, "Oh, your mother is sick" or something happened to her or something like that, your mind gets confused, it goes blank, you do anything.

Family covers a wide range of concerns for many crisis-prone Puerto Ricans. The cases that reflect the family's significance most forcefully do not involve real crises but only the remote possibility of a crisis. A Latin man may fear abandonment after one day without contact from loved ones; may feel profound discomfort at the prospect of being alone with thoughts of family; may become morbidly preoccupied with the possibility that harm will befall his family. The frequent statement of suicidal intent in the hypothetical event of the mother's death is forceful testimony to the centrality of Latin mother-son relationships.

DSH2:
Like let's say, for instance, today I got a letter. And if I was in prison, and if I was disgusted like I was before, and I was to get a letter that my mother died, and that's the only thing that I care for, I have made up my mind that

this is what I'm going to do. Because after her I won't have nobody to turn to.

Many Latin inmates invest so much of themselves in their families that the family becomes the background against which they review their life histories. For them, to be lonely is to be abandoned by family; to doubt one's worth is to question family commitments. To some extent this reflects the actual mechanics of family involvements. A man who fails often does hurt his family. But some Latin men find family connotations in what others tend to see as purely personal dilemmas.

The Burden of Close Family Ties

In the real world, a man can convince himself that he has options, even when this is tangibly not the case.[8] He can rationalize present failure by assuming future success. Free men may also find it easy to ignore the destructive impact of their behavior on others. This fact can translate into problems of guilt for some Latin prisoners (especially Latin addicts) because their criminal and self-centered conduct has placed a burden on their families. Family-related transgressions may eventually come home to roost in confinement, when the inmate is neither able to redress the harm he has caused, nor escape its implication.

We have seen that a sequence emerges among our Latin comparison interviewees in the shape of statements of regret and concern for the fate of loved ones who must now cope without their support. Here family links are described as two-way, and the man experiences guilt because he can no longer play required family roles. For some of the more crisis-prone Latin inmates, however, incarceration represents the culmination of a history of one-way dependency. This dependency becomes troublesome because confinement highlights for these men the unmerited support family members have given and continue to give them.

Thus a man may make the painful "discovery" upon incarceration that his mother, who always chided him about his delinquent activities and whom he resented, is the only person who will stand by him during his confinement:

ARS L:
Sometimes you even say to yourself, "she has no right to do this to me, because I'm me and she's her. Regardless if she's my mother or not." You start thinking these things. But you're robbing or doing anything, you know. Various things. But when you're uptight you start realizing there's only one person usually there, that's got their hand extended out trying to grab yours, and that's your mother. . . . You don't realize these things until, like they say, experience is the best teacher. When you experience these things, that's when you really know that the love is there.

Such continued unconditional family support and concern after incarceration, particularly from mothers, makes some Latin inmates feel impotent; so much is done for them but they have brought only shame upon their benefactors. For example:

DSH 57:

My mother's the only person. Every time I get arrested, she tries to bail me out. She does that much, whatever she has, she bails me out. She bailed me out two times before, and I didn't go back to court because I was too depressed after coming in and out before then. And everywhere I go, my mother comes and visits, and she starts crying.

Considerable ambivalence can result from the perception of one's dependency. Some of the more dependent and crisis-prone Latin men characterize themselves as victims of benevolent tyrants. They question whether the world—especially the prison or jail world—is one for which their family experience has adequately prepared them:

MSH 54:

The idea of me being a man, and I'm still living with them, and I'm like a baby, and still dependent on them for a lot of things, and this kind of gets to me.

DSH 54:

Well, in the cell you wake up. You think about the good and the bad parts. And your family and what they've done for you. You justify some of the things they did for you, and at the same time you disagree with some of the things because you feel that you fell through them sometimes because they didn't give you restrictions. You've waken up.

In the extreme, the disjunction between the family and prison can appear stark and unbridgable, leading to the conviction that one is completely ill-equipped for survival in confinement:

ARS:

Most all of my life I was with my family. We went places and did stuff together. If I was outside with my friends, my brother was with me, or if I was with his friends—we always stuck together. I was never too far from home. . . . I just feel that I'm in here, I could be doing time, [but] I'm so used to living with my family, you know? This will make me bug out, and I'm going to try to kill myself, that's how I feel.

Search for Parental Surrogates

The need for support is a theme that permeates the problems and crises of most of the Latin interviewees. Among comparison interviewees this need emerges in the form of a general expectation that the criminal justice system and its personnel should be responsive to one's requirements for aid in dealing with problems that range from drug addiction to unjust confinement. Such men espouse a "right or treatment or help" argument, and feel resentful when needed services are not delivered. For example:

ARS Comparison D:
> It's just that we got to be locked in. Every month just piles up deeper and deeper to me, you know? We can't do nothing. I try to see people to talk to. Nobody just wants to help. It gets me angry. I think I've got a right to talk to somebody and try to discover [solve] my problems. Nobody's come in to help.

The assumption that authority figures should "care" and that prisons should be responsive to one's needs is held with special urgency by a minority of Latin inmates. A recurrent concern of these inmates is an intense irritation with the day-to-day abrasions of prison life: slow and censored mail, bad food, "arbitrary" decisions and actions by staff, lack of interpersonal warmth between inmates and staff. Every inmate must endure such inconveniences, intrusions, and slights, but some Latins feel themselves unable to accept these experiences.

This phenomenon may relate to the issue of family. Some Puerto Rican inmates cannot endure what differs too sharply in prison from that which is available in the Latin family. These inmates may be saying to staff that if their family experience is not replicated, if they are not nurtured unconditionally and all of the time and on demand (as at home), their status justifies a tantrumlike explosion:

ARS H:
> You got any problem or anything about an officer, or if an officer don't want to let me do something, you cut up . . . when you want something you get it.

ARS Z:
> Like it's their job, I feel it's their job, and it's my privilege to get what I'm supposed to get. And when I don't get it I get excited. If I could get to the person who don't give me what I'm supposed to get or what I need, if I could get to him I'd just break wild on him, you understand?

Encounters with staff that feature Aid Seeking themes, although not prevalent, may have special connotations for Latin convicts. These men tend to define themselves as volatile, hot-blooded, and lacking in self-control. They may feel that in asking for medication they are asking for something that will help manage emotions and feelings they feel are built into their makeup. Self-mutilation aimed at getting medication may even, in extreme cases, seem involuntary and forced to the inmate himself and reflect psychotic (Self-Intervention) motives:

DSH 54:

And when I get uptight I bring my attention to an officer or a nurse or somebody, and I tell them I'm uptight, and I ask for help with some medication. And usually they sometimes tell me, "Wait for the doctor" or "you're all right." And they check me with a thing and say I'm all right. But I tell them it's not physical, it's my nerves.

ARS H:

First thing, I want, when I need my medication and they don't want to give it when I need it, that's when I think about it. And I say "no, I don't want to do that." Then I still do it, you know?

In their interactions with Latin inmates, staff frequently respond in routine fashion to what they see as routine requests. However, the counterresponse indicates that the inmates view their demands as nonroutine. For example:

CX 51:

I didn't feel all right. I wanted medication because I knew with the medication I would feel right. . . . So I told the officer "if you're not going to give me what I want"—and he said no—so I started cutting myself.

DSH 70 (Inmate Translator):

He explained when he was going to cut himself, before he started cutting, he has a razor blade in his hand, and he told the guard he wouldn't do this if you take it to higher officials. And the guard said "cut yourself," so he cut himself. . . . He said if they would have taken him to a higher official he would not do it.

Staff here have simply stated or assumed the obvious. Medication cannot be dispensed on demand by guards, nor can upper echelon staff be summoned to inquire into every inmate's problems. As Sykes has observed, such compliance on the part of staff (or elaborate explanations for failure to respond to inmate requests) would fundamentally conflict with the authority system of prisons.[9] These facts of institutional life prove difficult for some Latin inmates to accept, given their assumption that stated needs must be met. They underscore their premise by threatening to harm themselves and by doing so.

It may be argued that there is an element of coercion and revenge in such situations. The inmates see themselves as humiliated and abused, and their actions obviously cause embarrassment to staff, who must explain, if only to themselves, how routine situations are transformed into crises. Staff are also forced to respond, so that the inmate may see himself as having ' won." However, Latin men who injure themselves may not be primarily interested in revenge. They may feel that an extreme reaction is the only way to guarantee that one will be taken seriously, and that one will gain some response from the environment:

ARS Y:
He said he was going to call the captain but he never called him. . . . And I told him "I'm going to cut up tonight, and I'm going to hang up after I cut up." So he started to laugh. So he said "You're not going to do that." So I told him "watch me." So about 8 o'clock I started cutting. And he told me I was playing, right? I said "no, I'm not playing. When I talk something, I do it."

DSH 41:
I wanted to see the brass, high brass. And it just happened that I wasn't really getting the attention I wanted. You know. Officers say yes, and wait until we see one of them and then we'll tell them that you want to see them. . . . Now who knows if they're going to call or not. . . . (So) I did it, and it's just I did it because I wanted to get what I wanted.

In making requests, some Latin inmates place staff in a bind. They shamelessly express unmanly needs, and are a constant source of demands that transcend staff purview. Their requests are illegitimate. A man demanding medication looks as healthy as the next to the officer. A man overly concerned with mail, visits, or assorted (and often unspecified) personal whims may appear childish. The inmate, however, is forced to make bids to communicate that love and nurturance are really at issue:

ARS 1:
They said, "why did you cut up?" I said I wanted to do a sweet bit. I don't want to say, "Lookee here, I'm lonely, I'm homesick." I'm a man, you know, I'm not a kid. I didn't want them to get on me, so I didn't bring it out.

CX 51:
And you don't feel wanted. The officer gave it to the other guy. *The officer don't want you.*

ARS Z:
Sometimes I think that nobody cares about me. They just throw me in the cell and forget and throw away the keys, you know?

In Puerto Rican culture a request denied is an insult. The culture assumes that a man does not make a request unless his need is real and the person to whom he addresses the request is able and likely to comply,[10] that the act of stretching out an empty hand precludes refusal. Many Latin relationships founder on denials of such requests. Puerto Rican inmates may therefore be outraged when they belittle themselves by asking favors and are then further belittled by cavalier refusals to comply. Such inmates pose an unusual problem. They make nonnegotiable demands for care and love—then, if these overtures are rejected, they take a "supermanly" stance and defy their keepers. For example:

DSH 54:

An officer put his finger on me, and I said, "You better leave me alone," and pushed him off. And I said, "I'm just as much a man as you. Because you have a uniform don't mean anything." And he pushed the issue, and he put some handcuffs on, and on impulse I broke a piece of glass and cut myself. And I said, "You better leave me alone," and he said, "O.K."

These men vacillate from plaintive requests for special assistance to hypersensitive reactions when their autonomy is violated. This combination of anger and of requests for warmth, which is reminiscent of family conflicts, confront staff with alien dilemmas.

Some Latin inmates make an issue out of what guards and other inmates consider the givens (admittedly unpleasant) of prison life. A frequent complaint is that there is no communication with respect to the irritants of confinement. In fact, very specific and accurate information about prison routine is given out daily. Some Puerto Ricans apparently cannot accept the reality of impersonal prison life. For one, they do not see the real issues, such as warmth, to be covered by neutral definitions. Second, they feel that they are not taken seriously, which is probably true, considering the questions they view as compelling. Third, they may see the language problem as one-way, failing to recognize their own contributions to it. They may communicate less clearly than they are able to, then feel slighted when the message is lost. This takes an ironic turn when a man claims not to understand English, and then testifies to having heard crude remarks about himself or his family.

But it is equally true that prison staff do not appreciate the connotations of mail, visits, and medication to many Latin men. These inmates cannot broach their real needs, their requests for warmth and consideration. And the style of their demands promotes degenerting sequences. The men may push because they feel cornered or abused, and thus engender staff responses that corner and abuse.

Latin prison conflicts often stem from a need to personalize an impersonal environment; minor encounters become critical junctures: slights to one's manhood, arbitrary tampering with the necessities of life, failures to attend to advertised needs. Virtually every Puerto Rican in crisis will list such issues as open wounds that require nursing. When he tries to sew nursing stripes on his guards he discovers an obdurate (hence malevolent) system.

Sibling Conflicts

The comparison sample of Latin inmates typically experience problems which are more real by prison standards than the dilemmas to which self-destructive Puerto Rican inmates succumb. The more substantial family-linked problems experienced by most Latin inmates relate to actual threats to their family ties, such as is occasioned by a death in the family. Crisis-prone Latin prisoners, by contrast, respond to abandonment cues that are often at best indirect. The extent to which dependency needs influence the prison experience of the more vulnerable Latin inmates is particularly evident when we compare the types of problems each group encounters with other inmates.

In Chapter 4 we observed that one out of every four of the Latin comparison interviewees was confronted with a Fate Avoidance conflict, but that few Latin convicts injure or attempt to kill themselves because of peer pressures. The Fate Avoidance situations encountered by comparison inmates typically involved young black inmates threatening young Latin inmates. These situations were resolved or avoided by a show of force from the prospective victim, or by transfers to other settings in which the man had friends, or which were designed to protect potential victims. The fact that peer threats rarely figure in the crises of the more dependent Latin inmates may relate to the extent of their involvement with their families. Since their concerns are primarily (and sometimes exclusively) with the outside world, predatory peers are not a relevant feature of their prison experience. Except for a few Latin inmates who describe sequences involving face-to-face confrontations, the issue of personal security in prison is not on the agenda of crisis-prone Latin men.

To be sure, some of the more dependent Latin inmates do have problems with their peers. But these encounters are often fraught with family connotations and involve staff in the assigned role of parent-surrogate or adjudicator of sibling rivalry. This sequence is reflected in the concerns voiced by members of a Spanish speaking group who explained their dilemma to us with the aid of a bilingual inmate. Their translator records a revealing scenario:

Group translator:
> We are in Clinton prison now and there is discrimination going on. The other inmates say "you can't eat with us," and things of this kind. . . .
> So we go to the superintendent, and say "we've got to get out of here, we can't take it here because there is discrimination." Nothing happens. So we lock ourselves in and the guard comes and to show how serious we are we are telling this guard that we are going to cut our throat unless we get trans-

ferred. The man says something like "go ahead and cut yourself," so at this point there is some serious cutting going on in the stomach. The purpose of this is to call attention to the situation so that some one will inquire into what has happened and we can explain.

The resentment these men feel toward staff in such situations is not realted to whether staff did or did not intervene in inmate affairs, but to the fact that staff did not intervene on their behalf. Staff—these inmates feel—have authority. Therefore, conflict could not occur without staff consent and it is staff who must be blamed for it.

With an abiding, culturally inbred distrust of impersonal organizations,[11] these Latin inmates engage in futile attempts to hold staff responsible for systematic properties. Failure to take "appropriate" action is seen as lack of personal concern. An aggrieved Puerto Rican inmate may feel personally victimized by the refusal of staff to transcend organizational limits on his behalf. Such treatment suggests an unloving parent. "They" don't act, or don't act equitably, because "they" don't care.

Demands On Prison

Penal institutions present unique problems to may Puerto Rican inmates. Latins often extol the warmth and feeling that characterize their families, and they may wilt in prison because there is little warmth there and because prisons equate feelings with personal weakness. The "manliness myth" hits Puerto Ricans hardest not only because they may bring with them sensitive problems in this area (the "machismo" syndrome), but also because Puerto Ricans are men with roots. Puerto Ricans for the most part, do not stand alone, while the "manly man" is a rock that thrives on arid soil.

Many Latin inmates feel the need to be nurtured, cared for, accepted. We have seen with the comparison group that when Latin inmates are armed with interpersonal resources, they can endure. Lacking such resources, they may embark on quixotic ventures for symbolic rewards—approaching staff for warmth and understanding at one point, insisting on respect at the next, and often intermingling these seemingly contradictory demands in confusing sequences. In so doing, they may help to create further conditions they cannot accept.

Some Latin inmates mesh peculiarly badly with the psychology of prisons. Their areas of central concern—dependency and authority—are dimensions around which the prison is purposefully skewed. These men find themselves in a world that encourages dependency (and thereby raises painful questions of personal adequacy) while surrounding its clients with blatantly unsympathetic (and very unlikely) parental surrogates.

We know that some Latin inmates form supportive groups in prison, or establish sibling-like relations with their cellmates. Such resources do not seem appropriate, however, for the more crisis-prone and dependent Puerto Ricans. These inmates seek out staff instead, those with authority, those who can help.

Seeking out benevolent intermediaries is a tradition ingrained in Puerto Rican culture. The weak and the poor sought out "padrinos," men who would intercede in their behalf in a harsh economic world and who were available for personal consultation and advice. A padrino could never be a fellow sufferer. He had to be secure, warm and interested in his protege because of the protege's inner uniqueness. If a man fumbled, his padrino would carry the ball. Responsibility ultimately rested with the padrino. The man with a padrino had found a mother away from home.

Guards, doctors and psychiatrists are only remotely analogous to padrinos. Nevertheless, it is clear that Latin inmates often approach guards for human services they consider essential; they make unabashed bids for special consideration, and see staff as conduits to psychological ease. They may use breakdowns to punish and embarrasss the negligent benefactor, or to secure special benefits from otherwise unresponsive sources. These inmates proclaim that staff have something they need, are entitled to, and will go to extremes to secure. If guards fail to meet their expectations, the inmates may feel free to explode with rage and despair.

We have seen that the Latin family may simultaneously support and handicap confined men. Those Latins who link prison survival with family ties or who seek a family model in prison may find incarceration cold and lonely. Those who feel smothered by the unresponsive prison milieu may develop guilt or be tortured by doubts about their adequacy. Without external support from family or family surrogates, such conflicts often become unmanageable.

Notes

1. L. Rogler and A. Hollingshead, *Trapped: Families and Schizophrenia* (New York: John Wiley & Sons, Inc., 1965).

2. B. Berle, *80 Puerto Rican Families in New York City* (New York: Columbia University Press, 1959); R. Fernandez-Marina, "The Puerto Rican Syndrome: Its Dynamics and Cultural Determinants," *Psychiatry,* 25 (1961), pp. 79-82.

3, W. Madsen, "Mexican-Americans and Anglo-Americans: A Comparative Study of Mental Health in Texas," in S. Plog and R. Edgerton (Eds.), *Changing Perspectives in Mental Illness* (New York: Holt, Rinehart and Winston, 1969).

4. R. Fernandez-Marina, E. Maldonado-Sierra, and R. Trent, "Three Basic

Themes in Mexican and Puerto Rican Family Values," *Journal of Social Psychology,* 48 (1958), pp. 167-181.

5. J. Fitzpatrick, *Puerto Rican Americans: The Meaning of Migration to the Mainland* (Englewood Cliffs, New Jersey: Prentice-Hall, Inc., 1971).

6. D. Dandt, *Tropical Childhood* (Chapel Hill: University of North Carolina Press, 1959).

7. See E. Trautman, "Suicide Attempts of Puerto Rican Immigrants," *Psychiatric Quarterly,* 35 (1961), pp. 544-554, for the role of family in suicide attempts in the free world.

8. H. Toch, *Men in Crisis: Human Breakdown in Prison* (Chicago: Aldine Publishing Company, 1975).

9. G. Sykes, *The Society of Captives* (Princeton, New Jersey: Princeton University Press, 1958, p. 75).

10. Fitzpatrick, *Puerto Rican Americans,* p. 82.

11. Ibid., p. 91.

6

Slums and Survival

Coping difficulties among lower class blacks in the free world tend to reflect the impact of an arbitrary and often malevolent environment. Hypertension, significantly overrepresented among blacks, has been repeatedly correlated with an image of the world that requires a stance of alertness, tension, and readiness to respond.[a] This problem (hypertension), which some experts feel affects upwards of half the ghetto population, is based on the realization that one must anticipate adversity to avoid it. Since adversity manifests itself in a variety of situations, from social discrimination to outright attack, a person must scan his environment for signs of impending trouble. The result is a propensity to react to real or imagined impingements, and a consequent problem in the area of managing feelings.[b]

Coping failures, expressed in rates of suicide and mental health commitments, have been linked by a variety of researchers to feelings of vulnerability and fear. In Hendin's sample of suicidal New York City blacks, for example, fear occurred when the men felt uncontrollable destructive urges;[1] Breed traced a picture of southern black suicide in which fear and helplessness arose in reaction to arbitrary and threatening authority figures.[2] And numerous observers report

---

[a]For statistics on the prevalence of hypertension among blacks see: A. Sclare, "Cultural Determinants in the Neurotic Negro," *British Journal of Medical Psychology*, 26 (1952), pp. 279-288; J. Slater, "Hypertension: Biggest Killer of Blacks," *Ebony*, June 1973, p. 96; and R. Finnerty, "Hypertension in the Inner City," *Circulation*, 47, January 1973, pp. 73-79. Studies linking hypertension to a defensive world view include: W. Grace and D. Graham, "Relationship of Specific Attitudes and Emotions to Certain Bodily Diseases," *Psychosomatic Medicine*, 24 (1962), pp. 159-169; D. Graham, J. Stein, and G. Winakur, "Experimental Investigation of the Specificity of Attitude Hypotheses in Psychosomatic Disease," *Psychosomatic Medicine*, 20 (1958), pp. 446-456; D. Graham et al., "Specific Attitudes in Initial Interviews with Patients Having Different 'Psychomatic' Diseases," *Psychosomatic Medicine*, 24 (1962), pp. 257-266; and M. Kidson, "Personality and Hypertension," *Journal of Psychosomatic Research*, 17, January 1973, pp. 35-41.

[b]Feeling control problems among blacks, particularly of aggression, are discussed in the following works: J. Dollard, *Class and Caste in a Southern Town* (New Haven: Yale University Press, 1937); A. Davis and J. Dollard, *Children of Bondage* (Washington: American Council on Education, 1940); A. Kardiner and L. Ovesey, *The Mark of Oppression: Explorations in the Personality of the American Negro* (New York: W. W. Norton & Company, Inc., 1951); B. Karon, *The Negro Personality: A Rigorous Investigation of the Effects of Culture* (New York: Springer Publishing Company, Inc., 1958); W. Grier and P. Cobbs, *Black Rage* (New York: Basic Books, Inc., 1968); R. Crain and C. Weisman, *Discrimination? Personality and Achievement—A Survey of Northern Blacks* (Detroit: Seminar Press Inc., 1972).

that paranoia is the most frequent primary or secondary diagnostic classification applied to blacks.[3]

These patterns may represent versions (although admittedly sometimes exaggerated versions) of the self-defensive concerns that undergird ghetto survival norms. Hypertension may be a logical extrapolation of the self-protectively vigilant stance—both responses appear to share suspicion and resentment as a basic premise; both feature alertness and hyperactivity as behavioral manifestations.[4] Fear of one's destructive potential and the destructive potential of others may be a product of chronic concern with a hostile environment.[5] Paranoid breakdowns may represent the culmination of this pattern; suspicion and fear become extreme in response to imaginary opponents who are armed with one's projected destructive urges.[6]

Adjustment problems among black prisoners parallel difficulties reflected in ghetto coping (see Chapter 4). They show themselves in day-to-day concerns for survival in an arbitrary (Self-Victimization) and tension provoking (Self-Release) environment. We will see that the few black men who experience crises in confinement succumb to fear situations that are variations on pressures which evoke panic in the ghetto. Though these concerns are exaggerated and distorted reflections of ghetto problems, they have roots in a view of the world and in appropriate reactions to that world which are shared by many ghetto men in both the free community and the prison.

The Care and Feeding of Resentment

The suspicious, self-protectively vigilant stance with which many black inmates approach confinement makes the pose of victim (Self-Victimization) seem legitimate and supported by the facts. Black prisoners are able to point to a variety of conditions they feel are calculated to deal them unjustified harm. Our interviews with a cross-section of black convicts show that the victim perspective can encompass wrongs that relate to substantial injustices (such as being railroaded) or to the cumulation of petty confrontations and incursions by officials that are designed to emasculate and abuse. For some, such actions take on a systematic cast, justifying (and reflecting) militancy.

We summarized the feelings of victimization expressed by typical respondents in the following manner:

MHDM Comparison 7:
This man feels that he has been an innocent victim of repeated abuses, not only on this bust, but including virtually all the treatment he's received in the past at the hands of the criminal justice system, both inside and outside prison. . . . For example, he describes himself as being repeatedly harassed, arrested without evidence and by the same precinct on many occasions.

AUB Comparison 11:

> This is an inmate who feels he's been singled out by some corrections officers for harassment. It's a continuing problem of sensitive skin and it's painful for him to shave and these officers are constantly creating problems by insisting that he shave or locking him in because he hasn't shaved. . . . He points out that he has been the object of a lot of abuse, most of which is racial. His view of the injustice of the system is one of a fairly consistent militant type. He refers to the rebellion at Attica and you get the feeling that he was involved in that riot and he definitely conceptualized his degenerating encounters with guards in ethnic terms. For instance, beyond the premise of this sensitive face that he alleges he has, he talks about the endemic problems of blacks with sensitive faces being harassed by white guards as policy.

The view that the criminal justice system is geared to harass inmates is one shared by many black convicts. Some seem comparatively unmoved by this perception. But while most men feel bitter and resentful over injustices they feel are perpetrated against them, few see themselves as helpless targets of abuse, or as devoid of resources or options. The primary responses called forth by the experience of victimization involves striking back (physically or verbally) at the source of their discomfort. But this response is self-defeating. The legitimate target of an inmate's anger is either out of the person's reach (such as courts or parole boards) or is in a position of power (for example, guards). In either case, the offending party is capable of taking revenge. Expressing aggression thus offers the prospect of enhancing one's status as a victim.[7]

The sequence in which injustice spawns rage, which in turn must be suppressed or ventilated in indirect (safe) ways, is a theme we explored in our discussion of the "cool" role of black ghettos (see Chapter 2). An extreme concern for suppression of feelings and the appearance of self-control is shown by some convicts. They feel that in order to survive in a world that poses threats a person must equip himself with a "shell" that protects him from noxious stimuli and from personal reactions to insults. As is shown in the following interview synopsis, such persons feel they must become solitary men, callous and impervious to hurt:

AUB Comparison 3:

> Our man tells us that he's built an emotional wall around himself and he defines problems as nonproblems and he lets them roll off his back. . . . He says he can't be hurt, by anyone or by the criminal justice system. He also withdraws from most human contact and he's an insular man. He talks a lot about constructing this nonemotional shell around himself. And remaining by himself most of the time. And he considers this the only way he can cope both with the prison world and the outside world. . . . He de-

scribes the shell as a product of repeated injustices and unfair treatment that he has received in his life. He says in effect that he needs this shell to resist the impact that things might have on him otherwise. . . . It's a kind of philosophy of life as he sees it, and it's a very workable philosophy of life and it's evolved in order to cope with a world that requires that sort of philosophy. In fact he makes it quite clear that even when he walks out of prison he's going to be facing a world that is treacherous and where there is a lot of unpredictable crime going on, so he isn't going to be able to relinquish this stance.

A more common (and effective) response to feelings of victimization involves keeping one's cool and maintaining a low profile to reduce the chance of abrasive, self-defeating contacts with authority figures. Most black prisoners, in other words, come to terms with their impotence and strike a pragmatic compromise. Survival for them is not an all or none issue, in which one turns off the world and kills feelings in order to maintain personal equilibrium. Nor do such men advocate blind militancy in which one challenges—and inevitably falls prey to—omnivorous captors. Rather, these men take a middle ground; they recognize they have limited power, and they realistically assess the boundaries within which they can operate. The element of risk, the harm that may result from refusals to comply with prison routine, lingers as a theme that reinforces a posture of conformity. To maintain poise, many black convicts deploy a battery of resources, ranging from physical activity or work (which can distract and ameliorate tension) to peers who provide meaningful activities and supports, offer feedback on the appropriateness of personal reactions, or simply lend an ear to grievances. Attempts to "censor" staff may be used to break the victimization cycle or to air complaints. Primarily, however, a man must rely on his own capacity to appraise situations and exert self-control.

The perspective of an interviewee in his early twenties who illustrates these observations was summarized as follows:

ATT Comparison 12:
This inmate paints a picture of prison as a tension-provoking and humiliating environment. He sees himself as a survivor and his survival strategy is one of compromise. He tells us that although prison routine is degrading, you have to comply with it to some extent because prison is a violent environment and if you don't comply there's a high probability that you'll be beaten. . . . On the other hand he doesn't advocate suppressing a sense of injustice or passively taking what is dished out to him. He sees himself in a sense walking a tightrope and the tightrope has to do with issues of equity, power, and manhood. He is, objectively speaking, powerless, although he has some play in terms of, at some junctures, where people transcend even the limits of decency, he might surface the issue and try to get his

resentment on the table; and in some instances, he shares his resentment with his peers, who help him gain a sense of proportion. But by and large, he feels that his perceptiveness, his ability to control his own actions, keep him in a position of militant passiveness and survival.

He describes some of the young inmates getting extremely resentful about things and he says this is sometimes seductive, but rather unhealthy. He would describe himself as being aware just as the younger militant who feels all this resentment is aware, but yet in the sense of being more aware in other respects, because he's not only aware of the grounds for resentment, but he's also aware of his own need to keep his cool so that he doesn't win battles and find himself losing the war of survival as a consequence.

The realization that a person must cope with limited resources in contests that are often no win-multiple lose affairs is a lesson many black prisoners feel they have learned in the ghetto. This lesson applies to a variety of prison threats in addition to those that relate to assimilating feelings of victimization and resentment. The simple fact that a man knows from prior experience that women are fickle, and that the world is unjust and often dangerous, does not grant immunity from stress. But while the fact that a ghetto man views others with suspicion and sees emotional bonds as impermanent does not preclude feeling mistreated (Self-Victimization) or abandoned (Self-Linking), our respondents suggest that these perceptions may make it easier for a man to handle such problems when they arise. The following interview summary highlights this point:

ATT Comprison 5:

He is an inmate who appears to be a very cool coping type. He describes his previous ghetto experience making the kinds of difficulties that arise in prison understandable and they include that the world can be unjust and particularly the criminal justice system can be unjust, that death is a fairly common event that one has to live with and that people, particularly lovers that one leaves on the outside, are pretty much like one's self and if they had to spend 15 years away from you it's very unlikely that they would remain faithful. And in fact this would be detrimental to them if they did. He points out, however, that simply the prior expectations of these kinds of events and even prior experiences with them are not completely insulating. When one gets put into the equation it can still be difficult. He describes this in regard to his own sentence, at which he was outraged, and felt a strong sense of injustice and anger. And he also describes it with the death of his grandmother, a loss that was a difficult thing for him to handle.

Confinement, then, provides stress for which ghetto experiences are relevant, but the demands of prison often force men to put their coping skills to the test. The difference between ghetto and prison in this regard is one of degree rather than type. Thus while ghettos familiarize men with a variety of stressful experiences, prison, as one inmate put it, is a "concentrated dose" of ghetto life. Though prison entails bitterness, resentment, and loneliness, it offers challenges that can be seen as opportunities to sharpen coping skills and enhance coping competence.

The premise that adversity provides conditions for personal growth is espoused by many black convicts. This theme is saliently depicted in the following excerpt, in which betrayal and abandonment by a loved one (a Self-Linking sequence) provides a critical test of the man's capacity to cope—to "play it cool" and to maintain a self-sufficient pose:

GM Comparison 2:

His crisis revolves around a problem with his wife. He goes home—on furlough—to surprise his wife, to whom he's been married for 10 years and is understandably shocked to find that she's been living with someone else. Now as he sees it, he made the only move available to himself, which was not to play into their game. He didn't blow his cool, he didn't do something stupid, he didn't, as he put it, give them cause to justify what they did. He sees this as a hurting experience, as something that he had some trouble with, but he said he comes from ghetto streets and he's learned in prison that these things are what he calls "occupational hazards." In other words, he knew in advance that this kind of thing could happen. It was now a question of whether he could put into practice the principles that he felt he had learned. Briefly these principles are that survival comes first, no matter what happens life goes on and he has to go on with it, that in the long run it's his ability to be sharp, to be smart, that will overweigh any tough or blundering or stupid move that he might want to make. He says that previous to his prison experience, when he was younger, he could never have pulled this off, that he would have blown it. As he sees it, he went out and was confronted with a situation that was radical and shocking and that he handled it in the best way possible and on his terms, the only way possible. That in effect he demonstrated that he was true to himself, that the principles he felt he had taught himself about survival served him well, that he was, in other words, victorious. . . . This man is almost obsessed with the idea of becoming an increasingly good coper, and would argue that prison, in the sense of containing a great many opportunities for coping and a great many sources of information about coping, can be a beneficial experience.

Not all of our comparison inmates share the benefits of ghetto socialization, or can respond constructively to prison stress. Reduced power and autonomy prove particularly hard for some men to accept, and self-control may be bought at the price of deadened feelings and empty, insular lives. For others, luck plays a role in their prison survival, as when defeated men are intercepted at the point of crisis by peers or ideological groups (such as Muslims) who provide support and directed activities. There are some who, alert to the threat of peers, play out stereotyped cool roles and worry about whether (and when) the facade may cave in, leaving them exposed and vulnerable to attack. A few, whose defenses are particularly brittle, may live on the edge of breakdown. Resentments threaten to burst forth, eliciting fear of lost self-control (and of its consequences) and suspicion of others who seem bent on provocation. Scrimmages in which "manhood" points are won or lost become battles in which the inmate frantically explodes, inviting substantial (even lethal) retaliation by staff. In such sequences, which we summarize below, the line that separates coping and falling apart fades and grows dim:

EL Comparison 11:

He is an inmate who feels that a substantial number of staff are arbitrary and go out of their way to give the inmates trouble. . . . He also describes numerous incidents in which he finds himself on edge and very suspicious of other people's motives, in which he, receiving very little information, goes up to someone and asks them if they have a "beef" and if he's the right man. But at the same time it's not a question of being upset and looking for someone to explode on because he's apprehensive about what will happen, mostly, well, will this thing get out of hand? Will I become too violent? And yet at the same time he feels justified when these reactions occur because these people are, after all, prompting me and these people are really legitimate targets for what I feel. Now apparently once he gets tense, he can respond to a whole range of stimuli—people on prison tiers making an off-hand comment he feels is designed to make him look funny. Or during a basketball game after the game gets hot he finds himself more easily aroused than others. As far as we know there's not that many fights he's been in and he seems to avoid any overt difficulties with guards, but there are these points where he does become hypersensitive to other people's incursions on him and where there is a struggle to maintain an equilibrium. And at this point his situation is aggravated by the fact that he doesn't want to get involved in a violent encounter because he's really not sure to what extent he can control himself and whether or not one of these fights may not get out of hand.

CX Comparison 21:

His major difficulty in coping with imprisonment lies in a pattern that he describes as beginning with feelings of victimization, particularly by staff, which lead to confrontations or near-confrontations on a fairly regular basis with staff, and on at least one occasion has led to overt violence, a fight between him and an officer. Now when he has these difficulties with staff, this leads him or creates in him a very substantial fear that that evening or some evening soon thereafter, retaliation is going to be taken out on him. He describes evenings that he spends awake, taking such precautions as closing the cell window, putting books or other various items near the door so that when it opens he can hear them coming. Dismantling or planning ways of rapidly dismantling his bed for his protection and for weapons. And talking, literally out loud to himself, psyching himself up for what he sees as a fairly likely confrontation, and one he has very little doubt would be lethal but one in which he feels that his only, the only, redeemable element is that he might be able to take one of the guards with him. . . . Now his coping strategy, if we can call it that, or at least the reason that he hasn't broken down in any overt way that he tells us about, would be essentially bracing himself up for this encounter and trying to gain some vestige of dignity from it by taking a guard with him. Then, as he puts it, at least his demise would have meaning.

We have seen that for many black convicts the tests posed in penal settings are reminiscent of ghetto dilemmas, and that ghetto survival norms and techniques can often be effectively deployed to combat prison pressure. Assets developed in one human jungle transfer to another, similar jungle, and the fit between ghetto learning and prison demands seems reasonably good. For self-destructive black inmates, however, the survival game has been played—and lost—in the ghetto. These men bring to confinement problems that are products of traumatic experiences in the free world. Their attempts to put on a brave facade are unsuccessful because the prevalence of violent behavior in prison makes fear and resentment more difficult to control. Peers, rather than providing support, present a multiple dilemma: their aggressive behavior aggravates tension, and their norms condemn open bids for shelter—bids that arise, in part, from the threat posed by peers.

Traumatized by experiences of failure and danger in the free world, a small group of susceptible black inmates experience breakdowns in confinement that are among the most extreme we have observed. Prisons are dangerous enough to inspire fear in even the manliest of "manly men"; when prior experiences have forged a link between self-doubt and vulnerability—as we have seen (Chapter 4) is the case for a few black prisoners—confined settings can pose excessive threats.

Trauma and Defeat

Cells That Close In

Segregation, which is prison within prison, isolates men both from the outside world and from each other. Confinement is absolute and unqualified. A segregated man is very much alone. He is also paralyzed and shut in. Many black prisoners see segregation as empty and sterile, as a setting in which boredom may be punctuated by petty harassment from guards. Some younger, more vulnerable black inmates, on the other hand, tell us that these conditions create substantial personal risk. As they see it, the remoteness of the segregated setting and the helplessness of its inmates invites potential abuse. For some of these inmates, segregation takes on the connotations of a trap:

CL7:

It's a fact that they can do what they want to you.

DSH 34:

The officers can beat you up, spit in your room, and all this kind of shit.

MSH 5:

To be in the maximum-security unit was like the end of the line in terms of you being able to control the situation to any degree. . . . you're vulnerable.

An enhanced sense of risk reflects and reinforces exaggerated survival concerns. In segregation, hypersensitivity to threat is particularly self-defeating because it alerts men to dangers they can neither combat nor avoid, thus increasing their sense of personal vulnerability. Feeling trapped and resourceless, the inmate becomes a prisoner of terror, a victim of Isolation Panic:

DSH 34:

I had gotten the feeling that the walls was closing in, you know: . . . I had started walking around the cell, you know? And then I started going to wall to wall banging myself, you know, my body into the walls. And like then all of a sudden I started crying and shit, you know? And then I started jumping up and down and you know, I guess I just got—I don't know why, I was mad, you know. But I wanted out, you know?

CX 17:

If I started thinking I might get that same feeling that this whole fucking room is just closing in on me. I've seen pictures, spy pictures, and old Roman pictures, where you see people, trapped and shit and the whole room closes in on them. That's how that feels. . . . It's like solitary there. I didn't like being up there. I wanted to get from out of there. So I was willing to do anything I can to get from out of there. . . . All I know was I wanted out of there, man.

GH 4:

It was like Siberia. An empty gallery. You don't even hear nothing. So I had to get out of there. That was the only thing. I knew if I did this I would get out of there. . . . Right then and there, I couldn't wait until I got out. It had to be done right then and there. I couldn't put it off.

The conditions of segregation immobilize and inspire fear among susceptible men. Social encounters in prison can exert similar stress. A man who is intimidated by his peers may find himself cornered and alone, unable to escape from pressure.

Dead-End Confrontations

In prison it is difficult or impossible to implement avoidance strategies that may work in the ghetto (see Chapter 2). Minding your own business presupposes the ability to steer clear of someone else's business. This strategy is of little value if you cannot avoid the other person or if another person is trying to mind your business for you. Similarly, "shucking and jiving," essentially a stalling strategy, is of limited value in prison. The aim of this strategy is to remove oneself gracefully from a situation and to avoid it judiciously in the future. But in prison you cannot "shuck and jive" all day, every day, and expect to get away with it. Such a retreat option is precluded both by the physical structure and by the social norms of prison; it implies weakness, invites trouble, and does not get you far enough away from potential antagonists.

Thus face-to-face confrontations (Fate Avoidance dilemmas) may occur more frequently in prison than on the street. Prisoners who emerge unscathed from such confrontations or who are able to defuse situations before they assume a one-on-one character tell us that avoidance requires a constant stance of deception, role playing, and cool. Our synopsis of the strategy deployed by one of our comparison subjects to avoid trouble illustrates this sequence:

GM Comparison 4:
Inmates run the prison, according to this man, and this can mean danger. He copes by staying in the middle, by "shucking and jiving," by manipulating to survive. He calls this his defense system. He says, however, that this is a difficult role to play, that maintaining cool in the face of these dangers and around all these various people who are playing similar games creates tension. . . . That always being on the offensive keeps him both alert and sort of uncomfortable.

Peer confrontations are particularly troublesome for fearful black inmates. Their low self-esteem makes it difficult for them to appear unconcerned, to smooth over the difficulty, or to engineer a face-saving truce. Oversensitive to danger and prone to exaggerate the potential of other men for violence, frightened black inmates often imbue personal threats with life-and-death connotations, and perceive their opponents as insurmountable and implacable:

MSH 62:

> They put a note in my cell and say they're going to come and kill me, they're going to hang me. So I showed the note to the police and told them I didn't know what was going on. Because I had heard that they will kill you in the Tombs, people have told me that on the outside. . . . and the day before that they tried to kill another guy. They stabbed him with a piece of wire. . . . So nothing couldn't tell me that they wasn't going to do the same to me.

MHDM 15:

> So like I was trapped. So I got so confused and didn't know where to go, so like I said—this is it for me. I felt like it was the end of the world, what I was going through. Then I took and hung up. . . . See, I got into a pressure situation. Like this little room that we're in now, that you could throw some fire in here and the only thing I could do is just die.

DSH 31:

> I'm not a great fighter. I don't like getting into fights. And I really hate violence, as it is. And the thought of me getting involved with these guys, and no one helping me at all, really shook me up. I got an impression of guys really out to get you, you know? . . . the bad point of it all was that I didn't have it in my mind that I was going to get beat up. I had it in my mind that somebody was actually trying to kill me.

Perceptions of this kind—seeing oneself as weak and helpless and the world as hostile and dangerous—can make it difficult to distinguish between subjectively felt vulnerability and objective danger, and can lead to delusional fear. Selective perceptions of danger, however, may do more than substantiate personal fears and feed self-doubt; because potent threats are frustrating and degrading, they may also create overpowering, helpless rage.[c]

Engulfed from Within

Attempts to "cool" anger, as we observed in Chapter 2, develop initially in response to a sense of one's helplessness in the face of external threat. However, if the conditions that intimidate persist, resentment may swell to rage, and this may make the person fearful of his own feelings. Though this experience is shared by few ghetto or prison blacks, we have noted that Herbert Hendin sees this dilemma as the critical juncture for young black suicides: unable to control their feelings of anger, they panic and turn their violence against themselves.[8]

---

[c]A similar observation is made by Grier and Cobbs, *Black Rage*.

Some of the crisis-prone men we interviewed fit Hendin's description. These men feel hemmed in by cell walls or aggressive inmates, but what they are really afraid of is the tension they feel, which threatens to explode and to invite retaliation. Attempts to suppress (and thereby escape) destructive urges can lead to the feeling that one is surrounded by danger, pressures, and threat, and promote Self-Escape crises:

MSH 5:

Right there, I dug that I was losing control. I was getting ready to explode. And this is bad. Once you explode in jail—see a dude like me, when I start getting in trouble, I don't stop getting in trouble, I just keep on. It's like a chain reaction. . . . I don't think that I was sick. It just kept twisting and turning. And like I couldn't get relaxed. I couldn't function the way I wanted to. . . .

MHDM 4:

I begin to have all these negative thoughts about what happened in the past. About officers' harassment, that brutality thing I went through in '69, this guy that shot my brother up and put him in the hospital. . . . I sit on the bed, and these thoughts are hitting me. . . . This is when all this shit starts going through my mind. And, you know, like I may get up to the point where, you know, the least little thing might send me overboard. . . . I feel that I have too much anger and frustration within me, and I feel that sooner or later it has to come out some way. . . . I feel if I let it go too long, then I will become violent, and I don't want to become violent.

Some frightened black inmates doubt their ability to maintain an appearance of calm and feel their resentments are readily observable by others. To "play it cool" they are forced to deny their feelings. But this strategy proves unstable. The men can neither identify their feelings as their own, in any intimate or personal sense, nor fully accept a paranoid hypothesis. They feel frightened, confused, and helpless, and seek escape from this subjective condition:

MSH 43:

I have no kind of control over myself at all. I get emotional. I get so upset that I just go off. And it's bad enough when your mind is with you. You don't know what you're going to do or what is liable to happen to you. I have no control over myself or my emotions. . . . I sense something happening, but I can't really pinpoint it. It's something there, but I can't really figure out what it is or where it's coming from. Or what is it trying to do to me. But it's there. . . . I just want to go off.

DSH 26:

It's out of my control. It just takes control. . . . it just comes on—wham.
Takes its time. I observe it. I guess whatever it is in me just tries to be right-
eous to itself. Still I have some problem adjusting to myself because I'm
afraid of something. And what it is I'm afraid of, I don't know.

Men who feel pressured by violent urges frequently demand protection for
fear of what they might do to others or for fear of what others might do to them.
They are therefore placed in isolated settings. But, as we have noted, isolation
offers them no protection. It leaves fearful men walled in, feeling more vulnerable than ever.

Caricature of a World View Come Home to Roost

We have seen that suspicious, self-protective vigilance can prove functional in
ghettos and prisons because it forewarns and forearms men against arbitrary and
unpredictable onslaughts (Self-Victimization). This orientation may become excessive, however, or it may become functionally autonomous.[9] One surrounds
oneself with threatening figures to escape not only from external dangers whose
source is unknown, but also from one's own feelings.[10] In a paranoid (Self-Preservation) breakdown we see a last line of defense erected by a fragile self seeking
to find a concrete and manageable external threat.

The conditions that generate suspicion and fear among self-destructive black
inmates in the real world are selectively emphasized in penal institutions. Although in some ways less dangerous than the rural South or the urban ghetto,
prison pressures can be continuous and unavoidable. The routine preoccupations
of staff and inmates with power and coercion contribute to an environment per-
meated with danger. Ambiguous prison encounters, when viewed with self-doubt
and a sense of one's own potential for violence, can feed emerging paranoid
suspicions:

MSH 1:

Everything is said undercurrently. You know, like one dude whispers in
another dude's ear. But you know what's happening, you can feel it. You
know, like people don't have to open their mouth, you can feel it. . . . It
was scaring me to the point that I knew I had to hurt somebody. You
understand? And that's fear.

DSH 14:

They started asking about my case and everything. . . . I just wanted them to come up like a man to me. That's what I wanted them to do. I mean, you know, if I did anything, to tell me. . . . I think they were trying to do something to me, that's what I think. And it ain't no joke. See, I'm not scared of one man, but when it comes to all five and ten and twenty, I can't handle them.

The theme of danger also emerges among black inmates who survived prison tests. The backdrop of this concern is shaped by the perception that in prison more than elsewhere the person is not in control of his fate. A man may perfect his cool role and monitor his environment with great care and still feel that prison violence is apt to explode unexpectedly, claiming innocent, uninvolved parties:

GH Comparison 2:
I know that I control nothing. . . . For instance, there was one afternoon, just after I arrived here, there was one afternoon that some static took place in the yard here. What immediately happened after that could have very well erupted into a situation where I could have been killed. You follow what I'm saying? The doors were locked. Those who wanted to leave the yard could not leave the yard. But there was a man on the roof, a police on the roof with a rifle. So obviously I was not in control of the situation. I was just another inmate in that yard, indistinguishable from anybody else. I was just a figure in the yard at the mercy of whatever took place in the yard. So now if this had happened, this could have been considered as a crisis had something gone that route. But I would have been confronted with, here you are, here's the ten years from now you had hoped to be home with your family living a happy life or whatever the case might be, and here you are laying in this yard bleeding from some guy who shot you from the rooftop. And you didn't want to be in the yard in the first place. So everyday, from day to day, I realize that this situation can take place because I am in prison and am not in control of anything that happens in here.

Feelings of vulnerability keep many inmates on guard. Prison riots and violent encounters highlight and lend credence to danger cues, and may leave susceptible men feeling paralyzed with fear:

ATT 4:
The riot was over and I was a little nervous after it was over, but if we didn't discuss it so much it would have been just one of those things. But we kept talking about it every day and every night. That kept penetrating in my mind. . . . I got very paranoid. You know, very paranoid. I mean, everybody's paranoid, but I mean very paranoid. And I start figuring that people's talking about me. And so I just couldn't take it no more. I just bugged on out.

DSH 9:

> I was stabbed while I was in prison by a guy who was a real—he used to turn crazy. Upstairs, a guy in prison. Ever since then I felt like I couldn't move around and associate with people. Like I could, but I'd always be looking back over my shoulder all the time. . . . I started what they call hearing voices. And it seemed like people were threatening to kill me. I don't really know how to explain it. It's just something that happened.

The structure and climate of the prison provides the raw material from which conspiracies are made. Rigidly hierarchical and routinized, cold and impersonal, prison parallels the classic paranoid image of conspiritorial control.[11] Physical and psychological resources are subject to external control (by white officials), and therefore to manipulation; one's food can be poisoned, one's peace of mind can be disrupted. One can suffer beatings—even fatal beatings—under color of law. One is helpless to placate one's tormentors or to stem their abuse. Such reasoning may make one's impending execution appear as the logical—and inescapable—conclusion of one's treatment. Self-Preservation crises can entail a resolution to destroy oneself so as to obtain a more humane death than one anticipates at the hands of one's captors:

DSH 68:

> They tried to poison my food because I saw most of them in the back pantry. They started harassing me so much that I got to the extreme so far as I didn't give a fuck about myself. All I cared about was going, dying, and sleeping.

DSH 60:

> I never had no acid thrown on me, but I know people had acid threw on them. And I said before I let these people burn me alive, I'll kill myself.

MSH 48:

> And when they said "kill," that's when I really started running around my cell, saying they were going to kill me, they were going to kill me. That's when I started thinking about suicide. I said I'd rather kill myself before they killed me. That way I wouldn't have to worry about them beating me up. Of if they were going to kill me they wouldn't have had a chance because I would have already did it and they wouldn't be involved.

The paranoid frame of reference may prove effective in solving impulse management problems in the middle class world, where the person has some resources at his disposal and may be able to control his fate.[d] The gambit backfires

---

[d] N. Cameron, for example, notes that paranoid reactions are less severe in stable, predictable environments, like those experienced by many middle class persons (see "The Paranoid Pseudo-Community Revisited," *American Journal of Sociology*, 65 (1959).

in prison—as it does in the ghetto—because there are too many dead ends and too many situations that are hypothetically dangerous. The design of the delusion, which is the prerogative of the patient,[12] is preempted by the prison's structure and mores. There are few nonsuspect allies, and sanctuaries are hard to find. Escape requires movement deeper into the prison, to settings that isolate, immobilize, and control. Ultimately, attempts to escape render defenseless precisely those persons who are already convinced of their vulnerability. Isolation, from which there is no escape, brings them face to face with terror.

Manliness and Survival

We have seen that most black inmates survive in prison. Modes of adaptation range from comparatively passive compliance with prison demands to more active, aggressive attempts to manipulate and direct stress. Peers and other coping supports play a role. But the theme of self-control, of maintaining some semblance of personal integrity and "cool," permeates the world of black prisoners. This orientation assumes that survival requires a conscious, rational, pragmatic response to stress (see Chapter 2). Penal institutions, however, require documentation for claims of manliness and demand skilled performances of the cool role. Some men, burdened with self-doubt and denied the support of peers, feel deficient under these conditons. They become afraid because they feel that life's games are played for keeps and that men who are weak and alone are prey to the strong. These men cannot, and probably never will, survive without external support. Prisons—and settings like prisons—present challenges with which such men cannot cope unaided.

Notes

1. H. Hendin, *Black Suicide* (New York: Basic Books, Inc., 1969).

2. W. Breed, "The Negro and Fatalistic Suicide," *Pacific Sociological Review,* 13, No. 3 (1970), pp. 156-162.

3. W. Grier and P. Cobbs, *Black Rage* (New York: Basic Books, Inc., 1968); E. Brody, "Social Conflict and Schizophrenic Behavior in Young Adult Negro Males," *Psychiatry,* 24 (1961), pp. 337-346; H. Ripley and S. Wolf, "Mental Illness Among Negro Troops Overseas," *American Journal of Psychiatry,* 103 (1937), pp. 151-155; and H. Cayton, "The Psychology of the Negro Under Discrimination," in A. Rose (Ed.), *Race Prejudice and Discrimination* (New York: Alfred A. Knopf, Inc., 1951), pp. 276-290.

4. See: D. Graham, J. Kobler, and F. Graham, "Psysiological Response to the Suggestion of Attitudes Specific for Hives and Hypertension," *Psychosomatic Medicine,* 24 (1962), pp. 159-169, and B. Karon, *The Negro Personality:*

A Rigorous Investigation of the Effects of Culture (New York: Springer Publishing Company, Inc., 1958).

5. Grier and Cobbs, *Black Rage,* and Hendin, *Black Suicide.*

6. D. Swanson, P. Bohnert, and J. Smith, *The Paranoid* (Boston: Little, Brown and Co., 1970), and N. Cameron, "The Paranoid Pseudo-Community Revisited," *American Journal of Sociology,* 65 (1959), pp. 52-53.

7. H. Toch, *Men In Crisis: Human Breakdowns in Prison* (Chicago: Aldine Publishing Company, 1975) p. 295.

8. Hendin, *Black Suicide.*

9. A. Sclare, "Cultural Determinants in the Neurotic Negro," *British Journal of Medical Psychology,* 26 (1952), pp. 279-288; and Brody, "Social Conflict," pp. 337-346.

10. Swanson, Bohnert, and Smith, *The Paranoid.*

11. E. Hamburger, "The Penitentiary and Paranoia," *Correctional Psychiatry and Journal of Social Therapy,* 13, No. 4 (July 1967), pp. 225-230.

12. Swanson, Bohnert, and Smith, *The Paranoid.*

7

Odd Man Out

The sources of breakdown among white Americans are diverse. For example, the crises of affluent, middle-aged white men, who tend to dwell on occupational failure, bear little resemblence to the breakdowns of welfare persons, whose despair may reflect the workings of an impersonal and unyielding world. Irish and Italian-Americans, although both classified (or unclassifiable) as white, may resonate—and break down— in response to different pressures. Some tentative syndromes emerge for whites as a group, however, when they are contrasted with blacks. To be sure, white-black differences partly reflect social class. Differences in stress exposure and management nevertheless remain when class is held constant. These differences may provide clues about the shape of prison breakdowns among white convicts.

Most prisoners originate in the low income classes. Poor whites, however, may in general be less prepared for the pressures of prison than are slum blacks (see Chapter 2). Lower class whites may be confronted with fewer objective "stressors" than their minority counterparts. Rates of broken marriage, premature birth, and death among spouses and other relatives tend to be consistently lower for poor whites than blacks.[a] Occupational instability (and "achievement stressor") is also less likely to occur among low income whites. When unemployment affects lower class whites, it is likely to do so for a comparatively short time.[1] Stress mediators or buffers (external supports) are also more uniformly available to whites.[b] The result of these disparities is a tendency for lower class whites to manifest stress reactions that are often clinically less severe (and less long term) than those shown by blacks.[2]

---

[a] J. Bernard, "Marital Stability and Patterns of Status Variables," *Journal of Marriage and the Family*, 28 (1966), pp. 421–439; J. Udry, "Marital Instability by Race, Sex, Education and Occupation Using 1960 Census Data," *American Journal of Sociology*, 72 (1966), pp. 203–209; J. Udry, "Marital Instability by Race and Income," *American Journal of Sociology*, 72 (1967), pp. 673–674; B. Pasamanick, H. Knowloch, and A. Lilienfeld, "Socio-Economic Status and Some Precursors of Neuropsychiatric Disorder," *American Journal of Orthopsychiatry*, 26 (1956), pp. 594–601. See generally: T. Pettigrew, *A Profile of the Negro American* (Princeton: D. Van Nostrand Company, 1964), for a comparative survey of low income blacks and whites. Summarizing the literature on differential stress exposure among lower class blacks and whites, Dohrenwend and Dohrenwend conclude that "there appears to be no major category of stressor in which the rate (of exposure) for lower class whites is higher than for lower class Negroes." See B. P. Dohrenwend and B. S. Dohrenwend, *Social Status and Psychological Disorder* (New York: John Wiley & Sons, 1969), p. 137.

The crises of confined white men may to some extend parallel free world reactions. Their crisis pattern takes shape largely by virtue of comparison with other groups (when whites are treated as a residual category), and the severity of their breakdowns may be comparatively mild. The rate of breakdown, however, is often high for white prisoners. In this survey, white convicts seem particularly susceptible to crises of self-mutilation and attempted suicide. The interview themes associated with prison stress allow us to tentatively chart the parameters of breakdown for some white men.

The major adjustment difficulties experienced by white prisoners relate to Self-Assessment dilemmas (see Chapter 4). The low self-esteem that underlies these neurotic reactions reflect chronic problems for some confined white men. Self-esteem crises manifest themselves in preoccupation with guilt over personal failure (Self-Retaliation) problems dealing with degenerating relationships (Self-Certification), and fear of prison pressure (Fate Avoidance).

Assimilating Personal Failure

Some white prisoners espouse values that may be middle class by prison standards. They aim for producticity and see concrete achievements as measures of personal worth. They feel they should attain stable family lives, decent homes, respectable jobs. But the fact of incarceration, and often repeated incarcerations, conflicts with these aspirations. Imprisonment for such men can spark an assessment of personal career that results in the conclusion that one has little of value to show for one's life. For example:

ATT Comparison 14:
> When I got sentenced I took inventory. And all I had was a family a few years older, myself so many years older. And not a goddamn thing to show for it. I have kids to show for it, but they're mine in name only because I wasn't much of a father to them.

---

[b]Shields against stress that appear to be comparatively more accessible to lower class whites than blacks relate to stable incomes, family lives, and neighborhoods. Open selection of residential areas may also be more of a reality for poor whites than blacks. See: B. P. Dohrenwend, Social Status and Psychological Discorder: An Issue of Substance and an Issue of Method," *American Sociological Review,* 31 (1966), pp. 14–34; Bernard, "Marital Stability and Status Variables,"; Udry, "Marital Instability Using Census Data," and "Marital Instability by Race and Income"; L. Schnorer and P. Evenson, "Segregation in Southern Cities," *American Journal of Sociology,* 72 (1966), pp. 58–67; R. Farley and K. Taeuber, "Population Trends and Residential Segregation Since 1960," *Science,* 159 (1968), pp. 953–956. We have noted, however, that some sources of support, such as peers, may be more available to lower class blacks (see Chapter 2).

Personal inventories are painful, but they need not have destructive impact. Since a man is locked up, he can reason that however regrettable his past conduct may be, confinement prevents any real effort at change. This strategy can boomerang, however, because it sells the future short for the sake of immediate relief. The task of change is forestalled (sometimes indefinitely), and a pattern of failure may thus be likely to recur.

Our respondent (above) is typical of men who have used rationalizations to avoid coming to grips with their problems. He has a history of drug addiction and of "revolving-door" imprisonments. After each lockup he lets himself "off the hook," as he puts it, with "New Year's Eve resolutions." This scenario, he discovers, is redundant, debilitating and destructive. But although it is resistant to change, it is not fixed or immutable. Hard experience has taught our man that short-term problem solving is counterproductive. Older and wiser, he now supplements empty promises of change with a more sincere consideration of his options. His plan for change is premised on the need to produce results that will ratify his good intentions. Motivation and support for change emerges in the form of renewed commitment to conventional aspirations and goals:

ATT Comparison 14:

> Jail in itself can remove responsibility. Jail in itself can give you the reason for not being responsible. While I'm in jail what can I do? . . . You can use that as your reason for being in a manner of speaking. You used this for your reason for weathering the storm. . . . But it got to the point where I wasn't using it for my help. I was using it for my reality. I took myself in hand and said "what are you doing to do. You've been in this before and you bullshitted yourself and then you went out and did the same sort of crap, more or less. Change of time, change of circumstances, change of locale." I was still messed up. So I said "what are you going to do. You're no kid no more. You can't convince anyone on the outside because you've got to show, you can't say." . . . I don't want to come back to jail. I also want a family. I want to be able to hold my head up. Even when I went out on furlough I felt, even though my intentions were good, I know this, I felt about two inches lower than whale shit. And that sits at the bottom of the ocean. . . . There's not a wall between me and what I did. I've constructed another kind of defense between it. The defense is now my family, my future, a wife, me. I want things for myself now that I never wanted before. I always wanted it, but I never wanted to make the effort to get it. I sat down and I got very cynical once in my cell.

A person who holds himself responsible for his fate can find prison a setting that fosters growth through introspection. Given a change to look back over misdeeds, to take a long view of his career, a man may resolve to change his life.[3]

Stipulating personal responsibility for one's actions may result in other benefits for confined men. Shouldering the blame for one's criminal involvements, for example, can help a man avoid the conclusion that the criminal justice system is arbitrary, impersonal and unjust (Self-Victimization). Imprisonment may not always be appropriate or fair, but the scales of justice eventually balance out:

ATT Comparison 14:
> Well, I told myself that if I personally didn't involve myself in the environment that led up to my being arrested I wouldn't be here, number one. Whether or not I had committed a crime had nothing to do with it because (of) the fact (of) where I was at the time that I was. And my record. I had a bad record.

I: And this helped you?

ATT Comparison 14:
> It helped me to rationalize it, yes. It helped me to see it for what it was instead of what I would have fantasized it to be. In other words [instead of] being depressed and seeing the world coming down on me I would have kicked myself in the rump and say it was your own goddamn fault.

I: Is that better?

ATT Comparison 14:
> Sure. It's realistic. Whether or not I am paying for a crime I committed could have hurt me if I would have let it. But I sat back and said to myself, "what about all the times that you get away with." And sooner or later I had to pay. And this is the first time that I've had to do a state bit . . . that doesn't mean that I was arrested fairly or convicted fairly, because I wasn't. But in reality I can't beef. Because I was drinking the honey from the cup long enough. Now someone else has to do it.

A focus on personal responsibility can prove stressful for some confined men, however, because imprisonment may highlight failure and make constructive change seem discouragingly hard. To apply new-found insights, a man may need support and direction. This may be particularly true for men who hold themselves in low esteem. Self-scrutiny under the pressure of confinement (a personal setback) can reveal to such men a past comprising occupational failure, social miscalculation and moral weakness. The experience, for some, is overwhelming.

Men who experience crises in response to personal failure tend to emphasize their weakness, their inability to avoid dumb mistakes. They feel angry with themselves because they are unable to exert self-control. Prison provides a variety of stress situations that reinforce feelings of inadequacy. The inability to avoid incarceration, particularly when the offense involves clumsy conduct, or to conform to prison routine can feed low self-esteem. Problems that befall loved ones in the free world can also be seen as reflecting personal blame; a man may conclude that if he hadn't gotten himself incarcerated he could have played required protective roles. Such men feel they need to punish themselves (Self-Retaliation) for their failure:

CX 39:

> Like I was sitting on my bed, thinking about it, and I would say to myself, "what am I doing here, I shouldn't really be here." Then again I say to myself, "it's a stupid thing why I'm here, all right." Then I was thinking "tonight I got picked up," stuff like that. Then it just got bad and then I split over to the razor and just started cutting up real quick.

CX 48:

> I was disgusted. I know I want to make the board so bad, but still I keep doing all these things instead of doing an order that I'm directed to do. I have to satisfy my subconscious and not do it. Make myself like a big hero or something, to the officer. . . . And then I kept on thinking about, was I going to make the board? "Am I going to make the board?" And then I said to myself, "why do I keep on doing these things? Why do I keep on hurting myself?" Without even meaning to do it, but it always happens. It always seem to be there. Then I was just looking out the window for a while and then all of a sudden I just broke the light bulb and cut my wrists.

DSH 28:

> One day I got a letter from home and it said in the letter my brother was up for statutory rape and my sister was committed to Rochester State Hospital for observation. I started thinking about it, and I'm the oldest in the family of the children. And this kind of bugged me because I always looked out for them when I was out there, if I hadn't got busted, I could have helped out. But I'm in here and there ain't nothing I can do." . . . And the more I thought it the angrier I got. Angry with myself. I think that's why I cut up. I was trying to punish myself.

The most susceptible men have histories of unassimilable conduct over which they feel they have no control. Their (Self-Retaliation) crises reflect the perception that their lives are destructive beyond redemption. For example:

ATT 10:

> It was sex, young children. I was ashamed of it. I lived a double life. Everybody out there that knew me respected me. I had a good business, good family, good everything. But this was my skeleton in the closet. . . . It was

just a vicious circle. I'd go through this spell of doing this thing and then I would go through the period of remorse and I would come back. And the next time there was an instance or an opportunity, I would all of a sudden find this reservoir of strength and it was almost as if I was self-hypnotized. I would be locked into that circle again. . . . I'd get spells where my wife would be laying in bed next to me and I'd get up out of bed and go looking for somebody to hurt—for three or four hours—I'd come back and get into bed and she'd never know that I left. I guess some people would refer to it as being a werewolf.

Such men are convinced they are inadequate. Their reactions show them a self that is susceptible to collapse. Even minor obstacles can disrupt their lives and serve as proof of impotence:

ATT 10:
I was something like a personal setback. Some personal disappointment. . . . It was usually everything. Everything was negative. Even the weather. Nothing was ever right. . . . It could be a simple thing like I was supposed to play handball with somebody and I would overreact to this so much that I couldn't play. I was a total failure.

Attempts at self-punishment (Self-Retaliation) are sometimes aimed at deleting the trait or predisposition the person deems the cause of unacceptable conduct. Some feel they emerge from self-mutilation with a rejuvenated self, capable of chartering a more productive course in life.[4] Among the many who feel their faults are basic and unchangeable, however, self-contempt can reach extremes. Such men may make serious attempts to end their lives, ranging from efforts to deploy others as executioners to self-inflicted violence:

ATT 10:
Well, the way I was trying to do it. I was constantly getting in hassles with people in the yard. That's a form of suicide. There was one particular individual that I had a battle with that had a reputation of carrying a knife. No knife ever appeared. . . . I was hoping that they would take me to the wall. By taking me to the wall, I mean take me out and shoot me or hang me or burn me or something. . . . When I finally knew that I wasn't going to die, even though I hadn't gone to trial or anything yet, this was pretty much predisposed, I think that's when I really decided if they aren't going to do it then I have to do it myself.

Men who view themselves as inadequate and despicable often see little hope of constructive change. Their act of self-destruction reflects an effort to disown themselves, rather than to face and resolve their problems.[5] Their conduct (and their low self-esteem) often makes them pariahs among peers and places them beyond the reach of helping agents. They are thus forced to live with their self-contempt in an environment that serves as a testament to failure.

Transition Stress

We have noted that white inmates, on the whole, may be less lower class than minority inmates (see Chapter 2). Comparatively sheltered background experiences seem to make prison a more alien environment for these white inmates. They feel out of place in prison, and are subject to a variety of unfamiliar adjustment pressures.

Men who have been unexposed to peer-centered street worlds may find their assumptions regarding interpersonal dealings are at variance with prison norms. Some may feel like "strangers" in prison because their values differ so much from those held by other convicts. Forced contact with peers may be seen as entailing the risk of "social contagion." For example:

EAST Comparison 3:
> When I first got arrested, before I got arrested, I was very stupid. Very naive. I didn't know what was going on. I trusted everybody. And now since I've seen all this nonsense going on it's gotten so that I don't trust anyone and I don't want to know what's happening with anyone. . . . I don't enjoy their type of humor, when they want to talk about all the robberies and things they did to get here. These things don't interest me, you understand. When I say that I'm working and that I want to go back to work, they kid around and laugh. To me that's my life. These are the things that I live for. I don't mind working, as long as I have a decent house to live in and decent clothes and my family. These are things that matter to me. This is what I live for. These guys, I don't know what they live for. . . . Well, I'm trying not to become like everybody else around here. I don't want any of my morals or any of my values to switch over. I feel that my morals and my values here are above average. I know what I want and when I get out of here I'll just get back to the things that I want.

The problem for such men is one of surviving on a day-to-day basis in an environment that is on the one hand novel, but on the other unrewarding and boring. Since customary coping strategies and supports are unavailable, the task of adjustment proves difficult. The effort to survive in a foreign setting may produce feelings of demoralization, of being worn down by ritual. The person may wish to acclimate himself to prison demands, but feel that prisonization entails a direct threat to his values. Compromises may be made (or desired), but there is sometimes the lingering fear that it may be only a matter of time before one succumbs to prison stress:

EAST Comparison 3:

> I just try to get through the day. I try to keep busy in the yard playing handball. Usually I'll be able to get myself out of it or around it a little bit, even though I don't feel like it, kind around a little bit, and then I start to come out of it. But lately I just can't seem to get myself out of this rut. And it's a hell of a thing. I just don't have the patience for it anymore. Like working these problems out, you know. . . . Now you're going to laugh at this because it sounds funny, but I look at myself when I came in here and I feel so much older now. I really do. I feel so much older. But I'm losing my hair, and I really am. I'm worried and everything. Even my mother says when she comes to visit that I better stop doing all this worrying, and everything because it's starting to show on you. . . . I never think about killing myself, but sometimes I just wonder about what am I going to do a year from now or six months from now if I feel like this now. I wonder about it. . . . I keep telling myself that after a while I'll get used to it. I see guys running around here and it seems like it's not even bothering them, almost like they're happy. And I say well maybe I don't want to get to that stage, but I'd like to get to the point where I could just take the day in stride.

Such men are typically oriented to the outside world for support. They may variously rely on family, career, or community status as coping props. The free world, for these men, is real; prison, in varying degrees, is unreal. Some feel completely unprepared to cope with prison. Survival for them may entail an effort to block out prison impingements. In extreme cases, this may involve a quasi-psychotic attempt to reside physically in prison, while living psychologically in the free (real) community. Such adjustment modes appear tenuous and unstable. The plight of one white comparison interviewee, for example, is summarized as follows:

EL Comparison 7:

> Primarily he would describe himself as a stranger in a prison setting. He feels confused, tense, alien. He describes the environment and everything around him as unlike anything he's ever encountered before and unlike anything he is equipped to relate to. His resolution, to the extent that he has a resolution to the dilemma that he finds himself in, is to attempt to relate as much as possible to the outside world. Now he does this in some mundane ways, such as paying attention to a lot of radio and books and trying to keep a sense of the outside around him. But he also has a general strategy for survival in prison, which includes an extremely intense fantasy world, which he feels is quite tangible and quite separate from the prison world. So he can actually describe periods where he'll be doing whatever he needs to do to placate prison officials and to act like a prisoner should, and then sepa-

rately (although sometimes concurrently) he experiences periods of intense fantasy, a way in which he can relate to (his) people in a way that he considers to be not only real to him, but perhaps the only real thing that he experiences. . . . So in summary when he would look back over how he lives in prison now the element of confusion, of reality not quite fitting, seems to permeate all of his difficulties. He would start right from day-to-day prison living and go back to the reason for his being in prison and the possibilities of avoiding future incarceration and encompass all of them in a formula that would read "somehow-I-got-involved-in-a-confusing-drama-and-I-can't-break-out-of-it."

The comparison interviews suggest that many white prisoners feel somewhat marginal in prison. Among less prison-wise convicts (the adolescent and less experienced offender) marginality may be most pronounced. Such men become crisis victims because they are unable to obtain support from significant others (Self-Certification) or because peer pressure proves novel and threatening (Fate Avoidance).

Bids for External Support

Many white adolescents find incarceration to be an extremely stressful experience. They feel they need support from significant others to cope with the alien pressures of confinement. There is a difficulty, however, in that family ties may be weak or nonexistent. Many have survived in the outside world without family support and have allowed family ties to decay. When support (predictably) fails to materialize in prison, these men feel helpless. Self-mutilation may represent a dramatic bid to gain an unearned response from significant others:

CX 26:

I wanted people to see, my own people to see how I felt about this. You could say for attention. I wanted them to see that here I am, I have nobody now. Look at me, you know, I need you now, help, you know?

CX 53:

Since I had had no communication from the outside I thought if I did this maybe my parents would find out about it and they would probably start thinking about it and show that they care.

Self-Certification crises sometimes have a pragmatic cast. The man concludes that he cannot cope without support. When support is not forthcoming, self-mutilation is a backup means of securing responses. But such self-destructive conduct is not undertaken dispassionately. The need for support is painfully real. The person knows he has alienated his loved ones; self-injury represents an extreme move designed to communicate genuine distress:

CS 26:

> Well, you say to yourself, I can write a letter, and then you say what will happen if I do write a letter? They'll read it, but it won't mean nothing to them. And you say to yourself, well, what if I tell somebody here, and they write a letter home? Then I said no, you don't want them to think they're forced to write to you. If they wrote because people had wrote and asked them to write to me, they'd say, well yeah, this kid—I said that isn't the answer. I said what can I do to show them that I need them, and this was it. . . . I figured if I cut up they'll write a letter home saying that I cut up because I feel as though people don't want to help me and stuff like this. And then I felt they'd say "man, look what I done." And it would shock them. Like a person trying to take his life is not a normal thing, you know? It's not an everyday thing. . . . I just figured "well, this is going to snap them out of it, they're going to want to help."

Crises that reflect degenerating relationships seem particularly likely to arise for men who have maintained the support of family or friends in the free world through manipulative, one-way involvements. These men are egocentric, and expect the world to be at their beck and call. The fact that they have caused others pain is of no consequence to them. They find it impossible to understand that they may have forfeited the affection of significant others. When loved ones fail to make superhuman efforts to ameliorate their prison problems, even though they have done so many times in the past, these men feel rejected and abused. Their resentment can culminate in self-destructive conduct:

CX 37:

> My people, they wasn't rich, you know what I mean? But if my family hooked up together they could have done it. And I couldn't see why they wouldn'd do it. . . . See a couple of times my people did something for me. I guess you could say I messed it up for them. And I guess my people just didn't want to take that chance. I mean, like they say, there was a lot of money involved in it, you know? My bail was $250,000. So between my four sisters and my four brothers, you know, I see that they could do it, you know? They said, if we did, if he blew, we lost everything, you know? I couldn't see it that way. . . . I felt like I was kind of let down by like my people, you know. They said they wanted to help. But to me it didn't seem like they gave a goddamn, you know? And everytime I asked them about something, it was just a stuff-off. They had a different answer, they wouldn't answer the questions forward. And I don't know, you get kind of depressed, until I just blew. You know, I can blow any second, just like that.

Persons who attempt to use crises to resuscitate family bonds tend to view themselves as unimpressive. They feel that people will not recognize or respond to them unless they advertise their needs or coerce support. Some men trace this assumption to their family experience. They feel they were never really loved, and consequently were forced to "act out" in order to be noticed. Low self-esteem may make the premise that one is not loved difficult to disprove, reassurances notwithstanding. Another problem lies in the fact that repeated efforts to gain care and attention may alienate precisely those persons from whom the individual wishes to secure love. When such behavior results in repeated incarceration, it may strain family bonds to the breaking point. The person who desperately seeks love may thus find himself abandoned when he most needs family support:

EL 6:

It seems that my mother wanted a girl instead of a boy for her first child, and she got me. Whether that's fortunate or unfortunate is a controversy. And anyway she never really loved me, at least that's the way it was put to me, and I was always doing these things because I wanted to be loved. I wanted to be noticed. And all this time, I kept getting in trouble, keep getting in trouble, they were there all the time, to help me. And I more or less took it for granted and like I didn't really think they loved me, because of what was drilled into me. I thought more that it was they were obligated because I was their son. And after this last time, they just dropped me. And it hit me like "wow," you know? And then I started thinking about it. They really didn't love me, because this last time, they were here all the other times, but now they didn't come this last time, and they aren't there to help me. I guess they really didn't love me, they don't care about me. And I have nobody to care about, and nobody to care about me, you know.

Prison crises may replicate a childhood pattern of love seeking. They may also embody the resentment such men must feel toward an unresponsive world:

EL 6:

I started reminiscing, like I said, about girls again. I wrote down different girls that I had known and their addresses, if I could remember them. And I wrote some gibberish down there that I loved them all and they didn't return that love. I left a will, I think something like that. To the effect that all my money and everything be divided among all my people by the laws in New York State.

I:

What did you think you were doing it for though. What were you trying to say?

EL 6:

I think I was trying to say I wanted to be remembered, I wanted somebody to care about me. . . . I was hoping that it would stick in people's mind that supposedly had cared about me or were supposed to care about me. People I was supposedly close to. Maybe they'd think back and say "he wasn't such a bad kid, we should have done this." Some type of feeling, something. Because I wasn't getting anything at the present time.

Individual differences tend to be ignored by prison (see Chapter 1). This may prove threatening for men who feel impotent. Breakdowns may be used as a tool for force personal recognition by staff, and to prepare the way for consideration of "special" needs. Such incidents reflect variations on the Self-Certification theme. The person wishes to prove that he is important and worthy of note, in the face of evidence that he may not be:

CX 19:

It's either pity or to get attention, or just to get my point across to the people. Like whenever I can't get my point across, by talking or something like that, I just blow up. . . if you do it like that, cut up, they got to listen to you, they will listen to you. And you got a better chance to get your point across. . . . Well, I think that when everything starts to get on me and I cut up, people were like yelling "you're wrong, you're definitely wrong," and stuff like that. [After] they'll sit down and try to talk to you nice, try to calm you down, so you don't hurt yourself no more. And by trying to calm you down and talking to you, you can get your point across and everything comes out right.

GM 3:

See, like I tried talking to people when I got the letter because, you know, it bothered me. So I didn't want to do nothing, I'd rather talk to people if I could. But all the people I tried to talk to, various people, people that I thought could understand what I was trying to say, showed no understanding whatsoever, you know? . . . I started thinking, damn, what's the matter with these people? I'm talking plain English and nobody seems to understand what I'm saying. Or maybe they're not even trying to understand.

Self-Certification crises sometimes result in short term payoff. Guilty parents or lovers may respond to such overtures, and prison staff may placate the man who demands a hearing. As often as not, however, the message falls on deaf ears. More importantly, these crises do not reduce the pains of inadequacy the men feel. Rather, they reinforce the person's suspicion that he cannot command respect on his own merits. To get results, he must resort to extreme measures.

Buying Relief from Fear

Men who harbor doubts about their adequacy and resilience are likely to seek stability in their personal lives.[6] Such persons find change stressful because change entails new demands, and thus raises the spector of failure.[7] We have

suggested that the tests posed by incarceration seem novel to some white convicts. A prevalent reaction to prison pressure among white inmates, and particularly among younger, less experienced men, involves panic (Fate Avoidance).

Some white inmates have an image of prison which is shaped by inexperi-
ence. Prison for them represents an unknown—but threatening—quantity. They
may have heard or read that young whites are open game in prison. Pressure
for sex, which they feel is commonplace, looms as a major focus for fears.
Personal crises mark a declaration of impotence; the men know that prison will
pose tests they are unable to counter:

ATT 14:

There was the element of jumping to the unknown. Like God only knows
what's at Attica, right? And I had visions of some very evil things, you
know what I mean. . . . I mean I had heard about the riot. I had read books
on rampant homosexuality and of black predominance in prisons. . . . My
thinking was, "how am I going to get out of this?"

CX 34:

You know, like I hear the place is bad. You got to be pretty big to protect
yourself, to get through. There's a lot of faggots and all this. And I never
really thought about it much. When you're out on the street you don't
think about it. You never think about jail when you're out on the street.
It came [all] at one time, you know? . . . It was fears of where I was going.
I didn't know nothing about it, except what people told me about it.

CX 7:

When you're on the street you hear about so and so going to jail and they
ripped him off in there. And I'm thinking to myself, "these people are all
up on me. If they want to rip me off it's going to be rough on me. I'm
going to have to see if I can get out of here."

Fear of the unknown may make men desperate, and desperate men may
make desperate moves to alter their fate. From the view of the panic stricken, it
seems plausible that self-mutilation may bring relief from the pressures of prison
life. A serious injury, the logic runs, will evoke sympathy, and result in medical
discharge or change of sentence. The extremes to which men will go to gain a
sense of safety is an index of their fears. The presumption that prisons are not
equipped to routinely handle injured men or that judges release the crisis prone,
on the other hand, is a sign of naivete. Men find that suicidal behavior results in
considerable personal damage and discomfort, but leaves their fate unchanged.
At best, self-destructive conduct may result in transfer to other (equally unknown and threatening) segments of the prison system:

ATT 14:

I figured that if I did this type of thing to myself, they're surely not going to send a blind man to Attica, this was my reasoning, right? I figured they'll send me some place and they might even send me home. This is rather sick reasoning, I'll agree. But at the time, it was logical. So I proceeded to go ahead and do it.

CX 7:

I was thinking if I went and jumped off this tier—I heard a couple of guys talking to me, they were talking to a different crowd, "hey this is a lousy place; if you want to get out of here you can probably just jump off a tier. You'll get out of here." So I was looking at the tier. I starting thinking if I jump off the tier maybe I'll break a leg or something and get sent to a hospital. I didn't know there were prison hospitals. I figured it would be something nicer. Nice hospital, nice people. So I figured I'd jump and break a leg or something. . . . And then when I was in King's County [jail hospital] I didn't known where I was going to go from there. It was one problem after another. Just going in deeper. Getting out of one thing and going into another. And what's going to happen over there?

Panic, for most inmates, occurs in response to tests. Among the more vulnerable, peer games, comprised of teasing and ostracism, may prove unmanageable. The simple fact of exposure to prison living may be an overwhelming experience for sheltered men.

CX 14:

Like guys, they kept tripping at me, you know? When you come downstairs and go back upstairs, they start playing with you. And I just stuffed that stuff off, because I didn't want to get no ticket for getting in a fight or nothing. So I been here about 13 months and haven't had no fights, just stuff it off. But I just keep thinking about it and guys keep bothering me. . . . And I went to program and the same guys right away started tripping on me. So I'd just think about it and then let it slide. Go out to rec, play cards, and forget about it. Then another guy would come up and do the same thing.

CX 1:

Just at times, I feel like I don't want to be in population anymore. It just gets on my nerves, I guess. . . . Just being around so many people is what makes me nervous. I've been this way since I was small I guess. . . . Well, one morning the officer came around and I was shaking like a leaf and crying and I told him I just couldn't take it no more. I told him I'd rather be dead, you know.

Susceptible men, however, may invite severe pressures. The object of such harassment is usually sex. Young white inmates may find themselves to be targets of sex pressures because they appear comparatively naive or effeminate.

They may be viewed as defenseless by prison predators, and their response to overtures may validate this perception. But the stress to which some are exposed makes them break down rather than yield to pressure:

CX 24:

I was just sitting in my cell and this guy comes in and grabs me by the arm, by my bicep, and pulls me out and tells me to get down on my knees. I mean, you wouldn't know what that guy wants you to get down on your knees for. You can't tell what the guy wants, you know? But I mean I'm small, you know, and you see all these big guys, you hear all this stuff and getting taken off and all this dumb stuff in jail. And you've never been in jail and you don't know what they're about, and it just gets to you.

RIH 7:

They sent me to a block and I started being abused sexually. . . evidently my body looks feminine which I don't like at all, really. I mean, I'm totally straight myself and I don't like being looked at as a woman. I mean, I consider myself a male and I'd like to be treated like one. And so I started being abused sexually over there.

AUB 1:

They slapped me in the face and another one kicked me in the spine. And they said if I didn't give in to them by tomorrow then that's what would happen. They would bring me into the shower room and beat the shit out of me and force me. And they said if I wasn't forced, that if I gave it to them, then it wouldn't be so bad. So I couldn't tell the guard what was going on and I figured that the guard wouldn't listen to me. . . they thought I was going crazy. They wouldn't listen to me. So I thought I would just go along and do something about it myself. So I was praying to myself, saying dear God please be with me all night. And then when the gates closed I just stuck my fingers in there.

The problem of peer victimization reflects the inability of many young white men to play the roles required to obtain immunity from prison pressure. Avoiding peer confrontations, as we noted in our discussion of ghetto coping, requires considerable street sophistication and poise. Some young white inmates seem particularly ill-equipped to fend off predatory moves. They attempt to buy peace of mind by placating aggressors, a strategy viewed in prison (and in the slum) as a sign of weakness and vulnerability. Others, who have been traumatized by confinement, do not counter peer pressure at all. They become immobilized with fear because they meet threats against which they feel defenseless:

EL 5:

Prior to my release time these guys had me buying them cigarettes in the commissary and other items. And I was doing this to avoid getting beat up or in any kind of scuffle. So this went on for quite a few months. And each week it got larger and larger. And they were calling me names, punk and easy to bulldoze. I knew that practically everyone was taking advantage of me. .... And this particular day I was in my cell and these three colored guys who I had been paying off from the commissary came in and started laughing and they wanted to indulge in some sexual behavior. I was frightened and punched around a few times and I was sexually assaulted. I was deathly afraid of going to the officer or any of the brass, that I would be held back from being cut loose. So I just held it to myself.

CL 1:

I walked by and all I could see was black people staring out at me. And they hollered names and stuff at me. And then I started getting paranoid then. When I went in my cell I seen one night there where a guard opened another inmate's cell and 15 other inmates go into this guy's cell to fight with the guy. And this furthered my paranoia. When I was in my cell I had a black youth running by my cell, what they call a house gang—they work outside the cell—coming up to the cells shooting paper clips at me, "hey white boy and this." So it got me paranoid. And when I went to court, "you're going to prison man." In a little place smaller than this room and you got 30 inmates in there, crowded in there like animals. And there was two benches on each side, one on each side, and maybe ten people get to sit. Everybody else stands. Everybody's pushing and it's dark in there. I got really paranoid. They just kept increasing I guess. I was afraid to walk out there. I was afraid to do anything. I didn't want to talk to nobody. .... And this is my first time in jail. So it made me paranoid and all thinking about the sounds and all. It isn't like I grew up there.

An added liability for whites is that in prison they are a minority group, confronted with a dominant group whose members often espouse different values and play by different rules. As one victim of sexual assault observed:

ATT 14:

The population in itself is predominately black, which makes the situation reversed as it is on the streets. You're dealing not with the choicest of society here. And it makes it very rough on an individual who is young and white and in such a position not to do anything constructive at all.

Minority status may bring special liabilities in penal settings that house a disproportionate number of black or Latin inmates. In New York City jails, where close to 85 percent of the population is nonwhite, a startling 55 percent of self-destructive adolescent white jail inmates experienced crisis of fear. Most of these breakdowns reflect "racial" tensions. It is not uncommon in such settings for a few whites to be pitted against an overwhelming array of blacks and Latins. Guards, for the most, offer little protection. They are viewed as unable to control aggressive inmates or to aid potential victims. Descriptions of the dynamics of sex pressure in youth jails suggest that the phenomenon of fear may be close to universal among white inmates. For example:

ARS V:
> That was a population of mostly blacks coming in. They have blacks now that believe that they're god and we're the devil, so like they started wanting to get rid of us out of 2 block. It's been leading on and leading on and one guy has a fight with a black dude, things go on. So finally blacks want to roll against the whites, you know? . . . Something starts up and then you got to lock in, and you lock out and you fucking shake. You don't know if you're going to get jumped, you don't know if you're going to get stuck in the back from behind. I find most [white] people, if they're normal enough, they walk either close to the wall or close to the bars, or stay in a crowd, a crowd of their friends. That's the only way you can survive in this joint. Because like our population in here, it's ridiculous. We ain't got no chance.

ARS T:
> One time we were all locked out. So all the black guys went to the back, all the Spanish guys went to the back, and the white guys stood out front. So me and my cellie were talking about what happens if they start to roll on us. What should we do? So we said we'd get a couple of shivs and we'd try to stick them. If we see we're losing bad, we'll run over to get protection from the COs [correctional officers]. Then again the COs can't do that much, they're scared too. One hundred and some guys running out at them, they're scared too. They'd call the riot squad, that's all.

The pressures to which white inmates succumb reflect their inability to cope with novel demands. The prison experience of fearful men, moreover, increases the probability of future prison stress. Victimization, which breeds trauma, creates men who are extrasusceptible to peer pressure during subsequent confinement because their vulnerability has been documented. And since they (like traumatized blacks) feel they know the shape of danger, they may overreact to threats, falling victim to increasingly serious crises of fear:

EL 5:
> Going to chow you see practically the whole population with everyone running around. And on the way I saw the guy I had a problem with in 1965. And all I saw was his glasses and then I don't know why, but I really got upset. . . . And it was loud and noisy there. And it seemed like everyone

was looking at me when I was in the line. So I stopped dead. And the guy had to say "move up." I was in a fog. I started to shake. I felt like I was back in Riker's Island [jail]. I don't know how I got back to the cell. . . . In the cell my mind was right back to Riker's Island with 300 men all screaming. I put my pillow overhead and cotton in my ears. And this went on until about 1:30 in the morning. I just said, "wow, I've got to go through this now. It's not going to be like before, where you get out in a few months, it's going to be a few years." . . . You've got to walk with your back to the wall. It was Riker's Island again to me. For seven years.

CL 1:

And then when I got placed back into jail the paranoia came back again, because of what had happened a few years ago in the jail. I kept thinking, what would happen if this were to happen again? So I just slowly built myself up into the stage where I wanted to take my life. . . . I went into my paranoid bag again. I didn't talk to no one. I didn't trust anybody. I seen certain inmates beat up on other inmates in there. And take them off. So I started thinking, I can't go through this again. So I decided the best thing to do was cut up.

Marginality and Stress

We have seen that prison creates special problems for some white inmates. Among men with middle class backgrounds (or aspirations), prisons can magnify a sense of personal failure, while providing few supports for change. Prisons prove particularly unfamiliar and stressful for men who lack experience with peer-centered slum streets. Such men may find prison unmanageable because family support is unavailable. For others, power-oriented prison games are situations with which they are unequipped to deal. The picture for white inmates is thus primarily one of subcultural deficits, in the face of adjustment problems posed by prisons and jails.

Notes

1. E. Shanahan, "Negro Jobless Up—Why?" *New York Times,* September 11, 1966, 6E; M. Aiken and L. Ferman, "The Social and Political Reactions of Older Negroes to Unemployment," *Phylon,* 27 (1966), pp. 333-346.

2. B. P. Dohrenwend and B.S. Dohrenwend, *Social Status and Psychological Disorder* (New York: John Wiley & Sons, 1969); B. Pasamanick et. al., "A Survey of Mental Disease in an Urban Population: Prevalence by Race and Income," in B. Pasamanick (Ed.), *Epidemiology of Mental Disorder* (Washington, D. C.: American Association for the Advancement of Science, 1959), pp. 183-191.

3. I. Goffman, *Asylums: Essays on the Social Situation of Mental Patients and Other Inmates* (New York: Anchor Books, 1961); D. Rothman, *The Discovery of the Asylum: Social Order and Disorder in the New Republic* (Boston: Little, Brown and Company, 1971).

4. H. Toch, *Men In Crisis: Human Breakdowns in Prison* (Chicago: Aldine Publishing Company, 1975) Chapter 2.

5. Toch, *Men In Crisis,* ibid.

6. Ibid.

7. Ibid.

8 Perspective and Implications

Prison's Impact

Our emphasis on the "pains of imprisonment" as a product of the interaction of free world experience and the constraints of confinement may go one step beyond current formulations of the impact of incarceration. John Irwin, one of few scholars to systematically study the relationship between preprison experiences and patterns of adaptation to prison, suggests that prison adjustment reflects a primary focus on either outside (free world) or inside (prison) norms and values. He argues that each perspective results in a qualitatively different perception of the meaning of incarceraton. The manly or convict perspective is seen as a consequence of confinement, and as one that transcends real world or prison world commitments.[1] Our findings suggest that the dichotomy between free world learning and prison adjustment may not be as neat. Although Puerto Rican inmates retain a strong primary orientation toward the free world, they may not be able to assume a convict or manly pose in prison because this stance is alien to them. Instead, they may play out free world dependencies in confinement in an attempt to replicate, wherever possible, their family experience. And blacks, although they may typify the convict perspective, may not have to divorce themselves from the ghetto world to do so. In terms of the picture we have traced for ghetto blacks, free world strategies and concerns may reassert themselves in prison because incarceration duplicates many of the contingencies that arise in the slum. White inmates (as a group) show mixed orientations; their focus varies with their experiences in prisons and in the free community. Their prison adjustment problems reflect a lack of specialized experiences and supports that are relevant to prison survival.

The picture of the survivor in confinement thus emerges as that of a man whose real world coping skills and supports are compatible with demands of life in male, predominately peer settings. Unlike Irwin's classification, we tend to embody free world experiences in one coherent framework. This distinction is not merely academic; a holistic perspective on prison survival may have practical significance. Because if we are to promote adjustment in prison, and to respond effectively to those who break down, we must deploy coherent, integrated frameworks for analysis of the tests posed by confinement and of the resources needed to survive in these settings.

Ameliorating Prison Stress

Men who break down or experience difficulty represent an unnecessary psychological cost incarceration exacts from its charges. Such crises take their toll on system resources as well—men must be, at minimum, placed under surveillance, a procedure that expends time and money with no apparent payoff.

Currently, little more than custodial approaches to crisis aftercare are offered in correctional settings. There is virtually no research available that facilitates the creation of effective alternative procedures. The situation is bleakest when it comes to studies concerned with differential susceptibility to breakdowns. The significance of systematic group differences in susceptibility have never been explored in ways that might suggest differential intervention strategies. Our findings may prove useful in thinking of (and designing) tailor-made crisis intervention programs.

To be effective, crisis intervention efforts in penal settings may have to be geared, in part, to ethnic susceptibilities. Crisis intervention requires an understanding of personal dilemmas as they affect the person in crisis, and must tie to the nature of the individual's problem. Tailored treatment may be particularly necessary for crisis cases that reflect culturally linked susceptibilities because these difficulties are rooted in relatively stable personal predispositions which are reinforced by cultural values and norms. Some suggestions regarding useful interventions with various ethnic groups can be inferred from our findings.

Latin crises that relate to family ties (Self-Linking) reflect warmth and dependency needs. Short-term interventions with susceptible Latin prisoners may therefore benefit from direct family involvement (where possible) and from supplementary support from concerned staff. We have seen (in Chapter 5) that peers who play sibling roles may also afford emotional support. Long-term remedial work might be aimed at bridging the gap between family-based expectations and the demands of prison. Training for survival away from family would go hand-in-hand with the development of alternative bases of support.

For vulnerable black inmates, crisis defusing may require that the change agent address the assumption shared by many such men that the world (and particularly the prison world) is unpredictable and dangerous. Steps in this direction require, at the outset, the removal of fearful men from settings and situations that enhance feelings of vulnerability. Isolation is a common management strategy used by prison staff to deal with troublesome or brittle men. There is substantial documentation in our data (and other literature) suggesting that segregated settings may have destructive impact on men in fear.[a] Isolation may then have particularly harmful effects on susceptible black prisoners. We have seen

---

[a]A useful compendium of studies on the negative impact of segregation is provided by J. Rasmussen (Ed.), *Man in Isolation and Confinement* (Chicago: Aldine Publishing Company, 1973).

(Chapter 6) that fear solidifies under the pressures of segregation (Isolation Panic). The conditions of stimulus deprivation and immobility may bring home to frightened men the extent of their helplessness and vulnerability, sparking psychotic breakdowns (Self-Escape and Self-Preservation). Since no other custodial options exist to help or control fearful men, they may become trapped in escalating crises.

Prison resources relevant to crisis intervention include mental health personnel. Where psychotic fear exists, the services of a psychiatrist may be warranted. But prison peers may play a critical role in ameliorating crises among blacks. Peers are seen as a desirable resource by susceptible blacks, and they often play a central role in the development of fear. Selected inmates might therefore be deployed in supportive capacities, fostering trust and a sense of security. Some fellow convicts might function as "reality testers" for traumatized men; they could provide feedback on perceptions and reactions to help the man in crisis distinguish between objective threats and cues that were misinterpreted or imagined. Peers who share the experience of crisis-prone men, and who have survived or recovered from it, may have enhanced impact; interpersonally skilled men can serve as "inmate-therapists," who can bring to bear the "inside view" imparted by shared cultural experiences.

Peer support may prove relevant to interventions with some crisis-prone whites (as they may with some Latins), but many of these men feel alienated from prison peers. Staff may have more impact with such inmates. Change strategies, whether involving peers, staff, or family, must include concern with the self-esteem issue that seems troublesome for many confined men.

We have seen (Chapter 7) that some white prisoners are guilt ridden and resentful because they feel they are personal failures (Self-Retaliation crises). Support must therefore be geared to foster self-acceptance. After a man has been stabilized, the impetus for self-blame and self-punishment could be translated into motivation for action. The emphasis could be on equipping such men with the skills and self-confidence required for realistic aspirations and goals.

For adolescent white inmates, adjustment problems are frequently linked to the transition between sheltered environments and the harsh prison world. Since many find family support is largely unavailable, the focus of interventions must be on providing alternative sources of support. Counseling that provides insight into the manipulative and self-defeating roles many such men play might prove relevant to reducing rates of crisis. For victims of peer pressure (Fate Avoidance), bridging experiences to prison life, coupled with support from peers and staff, may provide buffers that reduce culture shock and yield a sense of safety. Unlike fearful black prisoners, many susceptible whites may require education in the ways of prison. They may also need a base of support (such as can be provided by peer groups), from which they can tackle new life demands. For the few men who are traumatized by prison violence, the availability of peer guidance may be critical (as it may be for some blacks) for deescalating fears and allowing a less jaundiced perception of prison.

The requirements of long-term stress reduction differ from those of crisis intervention. The goal here includes prevention. The aim must be to provide a prison environment in which a man's personal strengths or assets are allowed to operate in his favor.[2]

Hans Toch is currently involved in a research project designed to identify ecological differences among prison environments.[3] This project aims at an "ecological mapping" of the penal system that may facilitate the differential use of prison settings. Some types of "niches" in prisons may have characteristics that are uniquely relevant to culturally linked susceptibilities.

Settings that feature supportive prison staff or that are close to the inmate's home, for example, may ameliorate the dependency problems of Latin inmates. Some white inmates may benefit from comparatively sheltered environments, from which modulated contact with the prison population could be arranged. Reduced prison stress in such settings may deter preoccupation with personal adequacy and worth (Self-Assessment crises). The connotations of prison environments for black inmates differ radically between self-destructive and non-self-destructive men. Many black prisoners who survive prison tests feel they must contend with the problems of inequity and powerlessness (Self-Victimization and Self-Release). Prison environments that are comparatively open and unstructured may produce fewer encounters that highlight staff control and give the image—if not the substance—of arbitrary and abusive treatment. The possibilities for communication in less rigid settings may make resentments easier to surface and to resolve when they arise. Fearful black inmates, by contrast, may find such conditions threatening. Since they feel vulnerable, less structured settings may connote the prospect of unscheduled (and unavoidable) violence. Such men may require environments that are sheltered and supportive, and in which professional help is available to aid in the management of subjective fears.

Differential classification must obviously accommodate resistances to change among inmates and staff, as well as other practical limitations. Some obstacles to change relate to ethnicity. An awareness of different susceptibilities incarceration evokes for the various ethnic groups need not lead (and must not lead) to segregation.

Recognition of different meanings attached to recurrent criminal and non-criminal conduct may have short-term (crisis defusing) and long-term (problem management) implications for dealing with men from different ethnic groups. Armed with information about varying patterns of survival in prison, correctional managers may be more able to create differentially responsive and humane penal environments.

Notes

1. J. Irwin, *The Felon* (Englewood Cliffs, New Jersey: Prentice-Hall, Inc., 1970).

2. H. Toch, "Interventions for Inmate Survival" (Law Enforcement Assistance Administration Grant Proposal, 1974).

3. H. Toch, "Interventions for Inmate Survival" (Law Enforcement Assistance Administration Grant 75N1-99-0030).

Appendix A
A Note on Method

The Crisis Group and Interview Sample

The crisis group for which ethnicity is known includes 669 men. Self-destructive inmates whose ethnic background was unknown ($N = 93$), or who were categorized as other (American Indians and Orientals, $N = 3$), are not considered in this study. The identification of the crisis group represents the culmination of searches through a variety of institutional records. The aim was to inventory among men confined in the survey institutions between January 1971 and August 1973 those men who had ever committed a recorded act of self-mutiliation or suicide while confined. Data sources included medical, psychiatric and disciplinary files. "Critical incident" logs kept on suicidal conduct in one New York City jail (MHDM), the central office of the Department of Corrections, and a few prisons were also used to identify crisis-prone men.

The bulk of the self-injury incidents appear to have been reported by observers (e.g., guards). Some may have been initially reported by the victim. For example, a prisoner may have discussed an otherwise unrecorded incident with his counsellor or psychiatrist, who subsequently make the crisis part of the man's dossier. A few interviewees, however, mentioned events that were not officially recorded, although in some cases staff were aware of the incident. Six percent ($N = 6$) of the comparison interview sample described similarly subterranean crises, and were reclassified as self-mutilators.

A total of 354 inmates with at least one self-mutilation incident were identified for the prisons and a total of 315 were identified for the jails. Eighteen suicides (six in prison and 12 in jail) occurred during this period. Background data on these cases are included in the description of the crisis group, but obviously interview data on such cases could not be obtained.

Efforts were made to contact the 651 inmates eligible for interview. The earliest interview was conducted in November 1971, and interviews were continued through August 1973. A total of 325 interviews were recorded with the permission of the interviewee. Our relatively substantial interview sample attribution reflects the operation of a number of factors. It was necessary to restrict the interviews to men currently incarcerated. The flow of men out of the system and frequent or untimely transfers within the system (particularly in the jails) made interviews with many men impossible ($N = 279$). Language problems with Spanish-speaking prisoners who refused the services of a translator ($N = 7$), extreme psychoses ($N = 19$), equipment failure ($N = 2$), and refusals ($N = 19$), ruled out other interviews. Self-injury interview sample loss in the prisons and jails is presented in Table A-1.

141

Table A-1
Sources of Attrition by Confinement Setting in the Crisis Interview Sample

	Prisons		Jails		Overall	
	N	(%)[a]	N	(%)[a]	N	(%)[a]
Eligible interview population	348	(100.0)	303	(100.0)	651	(100.0)
Cases released or transferred prior to interview contact	87	(25.0)	192	(63.0)	279	(42.9)
Cases contacted for interview	261	(75.0)	111	(36.6)	372	(57.1)
Completed interviews	226	(64.9)	99	(32.7)	325	(49.9)
Loss from interview contact group	35	(10.1)	12	(4.0)	47	(7.2)
Loss as percentage of contact group		(13.4)		(10.8)		(12.6)
Reasons for loss from interview contact group	N	(%)[b]	N	(%)[b]	N	(%)[b]
Refusal	12	(4.6)	7	(6.3)	19	(5.1)
Language barrier	5	(1.9)	2	(1.8)	7	(1.9)
Psychiatric distrubance[c]	18	(6.9)	1	(0.9)	19	(5.1)
Equipment failure	0	(0.0)	2	(1.8)	2	(0.5)

[a]The base for all percentage figures in this column is the appropriate number of the eligible interview population.

[b]The base for all percentage figures in this column is the appropriate number of contacted cases.

[c]All of these cases occurred among "back ward" psychotics in the prison mental hospital. Such types may be comparatively rare in jail hospitals, because the more serious jail cases are shipped to the prison mental hospital for observation after they are determined incompetent to stand trial.

The ethnic composition of the crisis group and of the general population in the prison and jail samples is shown in Table A-2. There appears to be a dispro-proportionate weighting of certain ethnic groups in the self-mutilation sample. Latin and white inmates seem overrepresented in the crisis groups, while blacks comprise a relatively small proportion of the crisis group. However, some caution should be exercised in interpreting these findings. Absolute rates of crisis cannot be inferred from these data because the population figures presented in Table A-2 relate only to the daily count at the institutions. The total flow of men through the institutions over the three years of the study may be as high as seven and 12 times the daily population figure, respectively, for the prison and jail samples.[a] Estimates of self-mutilation based on official sources may also underestimate true prevalence substantially; the comparison interview survey (to be discussed) indicates that as much as six percent of the inmate population may commit self-destructive acts that go unrecorded.

It is also possible that the ethnic differences in representation in the self-injury group may be spurious. For example, these disparities may reflect differential release rates for the various ethnic groups. Data on average length of stay (i.e., time exposed to confinement pressure) for members of different ethnic groups in New York State facilities is not available. National prison figures are similarly unhelpful. In New York City detention centers, where the typical inmates is released within 30 days of arrest,[1] it seems unlikely that substantial differences in time served would occur systematically across ethnic groups. Such differences could conceivably emerge in prison. To examine this possibility, the average maximum sentences received by inmates of various ethnic groups in the prison comparison sample were calculated to provide a crude index of relative duration of prison stay. As can be seen in Table A-3, the maximum length of stay in prison (maximum sentence) is not related to ethnicity. Thus, the ethnic disparity between the self-mutilation groups and institutional populations is large (particularly for white and black offenders), and is not believed attributable to length of stay in confinement.

As was mentioned earlier, only 325 crisis cases could be interviewed. Table A-4 describes the ethnic makeup of these respondents in the prison and jail samples, and contrasts the interview sample with the recorded crisis group. As can be seen in Table A-4, the interview sample is not entirely representative of the parent self-injury groups with respect to ethnicity. There is a relatively high number of white interviewees in the jail and prison interview samples and a relatively low number of blacks among jail interviews.

---

[a]Exact figures are not available because official figures for inmates processed per year do not discount for recidivists. For annual prison population turnover, see "Characteristics of Inmates Under Custody," published by the department of Correctional Services, State of New York 1972. For population turnover in the city jails, see "Statistical Tables," published by the Department of Correction, City of New York, 1972.

Table A–2
Relative Prevalence of Each Ethnic Group in the Crisis Group and General Population in the Prison and Jail Samples

Prisons: Ethnic Group	Crisis Group N	(%)	Population[a] N	(%)	Absolute Percent Difference between Crisis Group and Population	Relative Percent Difference between Crisis Group and Population[b]
Latin	79	22.3	1,297	(13.5)	(+) 8.8	(+)65.2
Black	84	23.7	5,546	(58.0)	(−)34.3	(−)59.1
White	191	53.9	2,712	(28.4)	(+)25.5	(+)89.8
Total	354	99.9	9,555	(99.9)		

Jails: Ethnic Group	Crisis Group N	(%)	Population Estimate[c] (%)	Absolute Percent Difference between Crisis Group and Population	Relative Percent Difference between Crisis Group and Population
Latin	109	34.6	24.9	(+) 9.6	(+)38.6
Black	111	35.2	59.1	(−)23.9	(−)40.4
White	95	30.2	16.0	(+)14.2	(+)88.8
Total	315	100.0	100.0		

[a]Official population figures are derived from Correctional Department data on inmates under custody as of December 31, 1972, which is approximately midway through the research period.

[b]Absolute percent difference or percentage of population.

[c]No official data are tabulated on ethnicity in the New York City system. These population percent figures are estimated on the basis of a comparison sample drawn from the city jails studied. (This sample is described in detail later in this appendix.)

Table A-3
Relative Prevalence of Short, Medium, and Long Maximum Sentences by Ethnic Group among Comparison Prison Inmates

	Sentences						
Ethnic Group	Short (1–4 years)		Medium (5–9 years)		Long (10 or more years)		Total	
	N	(%)	N	(%)	N	(%)	N	(%)
Latin	44	(47.3)	23	(24.7)	26	(28.0)	93	(15.2)
Black	194	(51.1)	83	(21.9)	103	(27.0)	380	(62.3)
White	64	(46.5)	28	(20.2)	46	(33.3)	137	(22.4)
Total	302	(49.5)	134	(22.0)	174	(28.5)	610	(99.9)

Note: Chi^2 = 2.50.
Contingency Coefficient = 0.06.
Probability of Occurrence = 0.64.

Table A–4
Crisis Interview Sample and Overall Crisis Group by Setting and Ethnicity

Prisons: Ethnic Group	Overall Crisis Group		Interviewed		Absolute Percent Difference between the Overall Crisis Group and the Interviewed Group	Percentage of Crisis Group Interviewed
	N	(%)	N	(%)		
Latin	79	22.3	42	18.6	(–)3.7	53.2
Black	84	23.7	47	20.8	(–)2.9	56.0
White	191	53.9	137	60.6	(+)6.7	71.7
Total	354	99.9	226	100.0	13.3	

Jails: Ethnic Group	Overall Crisis Group		Interviewed		Absolute Percent Difference between the Overall Crisis Group and the Interviewed Group	Percentage of Crisis Group Interviewed
	N	(%)	N	(%)		
Latin	109	34.6	31	31.3	(–)3.3	28.4
Black	111	35.2	27	27.3	(–)7.9	24.3
White	95	30.2	41	41.4	(+)11.2	43.2
Total	315	100.0	99	100.0	22.4	

Data on rates of interview completion, depicted in Table A-5, show that the overrepresentation of white interviewees in the samples stems from a high interview contact rate for this group. Blacks, on the other hand, were contacted at a comparatively low rate in the jails. For Latin inmates, language problems reduce the interview rate in the prison. The interview rates are generally quite high, however, and there are sufficient interviewees from each cultural group to allow for adjustments in analysis.

The Comparison Sample

Information on prisoners without recorded incidents of self-destructive breakdowns in jails or prisons was collected on a weighted sample of 610 prison inmates and a weighted sample of 1,538 jail inmates for whom data on ethnicity was available. The sampling frame for the prison comparison sample was all men who were resident in a maximum security prison (or Coxsackie, the prison youth facility) during June and July of 1973. A sample was drawn from the jails surveyed for each year of the study to control for variations on demographic and other background indices that might arise from the rapid population turnover of New York City jails.[b]

Stratification by ethnic group was introduced for the maximum security prisons to avoid the large sample otherwise required to yield enough Latin and white inmates for comparison with the crisis sample. Since the comparison sample was drawn prior to analysis of the self-injury data, the sample could not be matched with the crisis group. As a compromise solution, approximately equal representation of each ethnic group in the comparison sample was sought. The following sampling procedure was employed to achieve this result: (1) Each prison was identified as a separate strata; (2) a systematic random sample of inmates (a seven percent sample) was obtained from each strata; (3) the ethnic identification of members in the seven percent random sample was determined, and the group was divided into subgroups of Latins, blacks, and whites; (4) different sampling percentages were applied to the members of the various ethnic subgroups (100 percent for Latins, 80 percent for whites, and 33 percent for blacks) and the members were selected randomly within each of the latter two subgroups. Stratification was not introduced in the prison youth facility because the proportion of the overall sample that would be comprised of Coxsackie inmates was negligible (six percent), and because official population figures indicated a small random sample would contain a sufficient number of Latin and

---

[b]As noted earlier, the confinement hospitals (MSH and RIH) were employed solely as resources to facilitate the location and interviewing of men who had injured themselves in *other* settings. Therefore neither of the hospitals is included in the comparison survey.

Table A-5
Crisis Interview Completion Rates by Ethnic Group in the Prison and Jail Samples

	Prison Sample					
	Latin		Black		White	
	N	(%)[a]	N	(%)[a]	N	(%)[a]
Identified Cases	79	(100.0)	84	(100.0)	191	(100.0)
Cases released, transferred, or otherwise unavailable for interview	25	(31.6)	27	(32.1)	41	(21.5)
Cases contacted for interview	54	(68.3)	57	(67.9)	150	(78.5)
Completed interviews	42	(53.2)	47	(55.9)	137	(71.7)
Loss as percentage of contact group		(22.2)		(17.5)		(8.7)
	N	(%)[b]	N	(%)[b]	N	(%)[b]
Reason for loss from interview contact group						
Refusal	2	(3.7)	3	(5.3)	7	(4.7)
Language barrier	5	(9.3)	0	(.0)	0	(0.0)
Psychiatric disturbance	5	(9.3)	7	(12.3)	6	(4.0)

Table A-5—Continued

	Jail Sample					
	Latin		Black		White	
	N	(%)[a]	N	(%)[a]	N	(%)[a]
Identified Cases	109	(100.0)	111	(100.0)	95	(100.0)
Cases released, transferred, or otherwise unavailable for interview	74	(67.9)	82	(73.9)	50	(53.7)
Cases contacted for interview	35	(32.1)	29	(26.1)	45	(46.3)
Completed interviews	31	(28.4)	27	(24.3)	41	(43.2)
Loss as percentage of contact group		(11.4)		(6.9)		(8.9)
Reason for loss from contact interview group	N	(%)[b]	N	(%)[b]	N	(%)[b]
Refusal	2	(5.7)	2	(6.9)	3	(6.6)
Language barrier	2	(5.7)	0	(0.0)	0	(0.0)
Psychiatric disturbance	0	(0.0)	0	(0.0)	1	(2.2)

[a]The base for all percentage figures in this column is the appropriate number of the identified case population.

[b]The base for all percentage figures in this column is the appropriate number of contacted cases.

white inmates to approximate the ethnic composition of the crisis group. The results of ethnic stratification in the prisons is presented in Table A-6.

Stratification by ethnic group was ruled out for the jail sample because there were no population figures available from which to derive sampling percentages. A large systematic random sample comprising 14 percent of the average daily census of the jails surveyed was drawn from each year of the study to obtain a representative sample of the jails and a large enough number of men from each ethnic category. The youth detention center (ARS) is weighed by a factor of 1.6 to reflect the proportionate representation of adolescents in the jail sample.

The weighted jail sample (N = 1,583) contains 394 (24.9 percent) Latin, 935 (59.1 percent) black, and 254 (16 percent) white inmates. There are no population figures available to assess the representativeness of this sample. However, the size of the sample, and the fact that the sample spans the entire three years of the study, suggests that it is probably representative.

The Comparison Interview Sample

The comparison interview sample represents a subsample from the stratified random sample of comparison inmates selected from the prisons and jails. The aim was to interview a disproportionate number of men from high-risk (vulnerable) groups. Stratification by ethnic group was employed among prison interviewees to ensure roughly equivalent samples of men from each ethnic group (33 percent for Latin and white inmates, and 25 percent for black inmates). This procedure allows for a more thorough analysis of the problems of Latin and white inmates, risk groups that would otherwise represent a minority of an unmodified random sample. Since ethnic stratification could not be achieved in the jails, disproportionate comparison interview samples were drawn from special housing tiers (such as drug detoxification and segregation units).[c] The assumption was that men in these areas might experience problems of adjustment that were more marked than men in the general population, and might therefore be more comparable on cultural background (and other risk factors) to crisis-prone men. The interview refusal rate among comparison inmates for both prisons and jails combined was 17.8 percent (N = 36).

---

[c]Because of the high turnover of detainees in jail, and because of the limited ability of staff to retrieve men from different floors of each institution, a comparison interview sample was drawn from each floor of the jails studied. Since there was more than one floor for the general population, a small sample from each floor was sufficient to yield a sizeable interview sample. There is only one floor for men under mental observation or segregation, however, and each floor holds a small number of men. Because these "special" floors appeared to be overrepresented in the self-injury sample when the comparison sample was drawn, enough cases were interviewed from each such floor to allow comparison with the self-injury group and interview sample.

Table A-6
Stratified Prison Comparison Sample

	Latin		Black		White		Total	
	N	(%)	N	(%)	N	(%)	N	(%)
Official population figures (as of 12/31/72)	1,297	(13.5)	5,546	(58.0)	2,712	(28.4)	9,555	(100)
Stratified sample (7%) (drawn between 7/1/73 and 9/1/73)	93	(15.2)	380	(62.3)	137	(22.5)	610	(100)
Sampling percentage	(100%)		(33.3%)		(80%)			
Sample for data collection	93	(28.2)	127	(38.5)	110	(33.3)	330	(100)

Note: There is a disparity between the prison population figures and the stratified seven percent random shown in this table. This difference is partly related to population shrinkage during the six-month interval between the tabulation of official figures and the drawing of the comparison sample. Population loss may have occurred at a somewhat higher rate for white inmates than others. Sampling error may also partially account for the discrepancies noted. It should be stressed, however, that the goal of stratification was only to approximate population parameters while yielding random samples of each ethnic group. The small error in sampling can be compensated for by using population figures to estimate the risk of self-injury in prison for ethnic groups (and some other variables). However, the main focus of the analysis is on within-group differences, particularly as they relate to the distribution of interview content. The separate ethnic samples should be adequate for this purpose.

The interview completion rates for prison comparison inmates are presented for each ethnic group in Table A-7. This table indicates that the obtained interview sample differs from the expected sample. Some of the discrepancy is accounted for by interviewees who discussed self-mutilation incidents, requiring that the interviews be placed in the crisis sample. The major source of disparity reflects limited resources, which dictated that some interviews be discarded. The interviews conducted at one prison (or sample strata) were selected for deletion from the sample because the tape recordings were virtually inaudible and would have required considerable time and effort to analyze. Since the prisons were sampled independently, the bias introduced by systematic information loss should be minimized. Ethnic stratification of the remaining prisons included in the interview sampling frame resulted in equal representation of each ethnic group and the desired overrepresentation of Latin and white inmates, the ethnic risk groups.

Data on interview completion rates for the various ethnic groups are not available for the jail sample.[d] The utility of the jail sample for exploring ethnic risk groups can be assessed by comparing the ethnic distribution of the interview sample to the general detention population. The sampling effort in the jails, which was expected to produce a disproportionate sample of Latin and white inmates, can be seen in Table A-8 to have resulted in an overrepresentation of Latin inmates only, and a corresponding underrepresentation of white inmates. The dearth of white interviewees in the jail sample may reflect the fact that the samples from each jail tier had to be drawn on a daily basis, and may have been subject to irregular population shifts. Differential refusal rates may partially account for this disparity. It is also possible that the assumption that stress exposure would directly correlate with self-injury breakdowns was inaccurate. In any case, comparative analysis of interviews among self-destructive and non-destructive white inmates must be largely restricted to prison inmates.

Background Indexes

Information derived from interviews (see Chapter 3) comprises the core of our data base. Background data was also collected from institutional files on all subjects of the research endeavor. Background indices include, in addition to ethnicity, nine demographic items and eight items relating to criminal conduct and confinement experience. Data on inmate career (rates of visits, infractions, and psychiatric contacts) proved unavailable for the bulk of the inmates.

---

[d]The total interviewed group for the jails is known (67), as is the number of men who refused an interview (32, or 32.2%). But information on ethnic background among refusals, and about the number (and ethnicity) of men who were contacted but not interviewed for any of a variety of reasons, has subsequently been misplaced.

Table A-7

Interview Completion Rates for Prison Comparison Inmates by Ethnic Group

Data	Latin		Black		White		Total	
	N	(%)	N	(%)	N	(%)	N	(%)
Data collection group	93	(15.2)	127	(62.3)	110	(22.4)	330	(100)
Interview sampling percentage		(33)		(25)		(33)		
Expected interview group	31	(31)	32	(32)	37	(37)	100	(100)
Contacted interview group	31	(31)	32	(32)	37	(37)	100	(100)
Obtained interview group	26	(33.3)	26	(33.3)	26	(33.3)	78	(78)
Source of disparity between expected and obtained groups (percents based on contacted group:)								
Refusals	1	(3.2)	1	(3.1)	2	(5.4)	4	(4)
Discarded interviews	3	(9.7)	4	(12.5)	7	(18.9)	17	(17)
Interviews transferred to self-injury sample	1	(3.2)	1	(3.1)	2	(5.4)	4	(4)

Table A-8
Jail Comparison Interview Sample and General Population by Ethnicity

Ethnic Group	Comparison Interview Sample		Population Estimates		Percent Differences between Interview and Population
	(N)	(%)	(N)	(%)	
Latin	22	(32.8)	394	(24.9)	+(7.9)
Black	40	(59.7)	935	(59.1)	+(0.6)
White	5	(7.5)	254	(16.0)	–(8.5)
	67	(100.0)	1,583	(100.0)	17

The 17 background variables selected from prison records are presented in Tables A-9 and A-10, along with classification categories used for coding and analysis. The variables are cast in dichotomous (either/or) form for analytic purposes because the small size of the ethnic interview samples (the main focus of analysis) requires conservative classifications. If data on residence, for example, were analyzed as a six-category variable (see Table A-9), there would be too few cases in each cell to make results meaningful.

Dichotomous classifications do not do injustice to the data. There is considerable information decay in prisons, and data in institutional files are often missing or incomplete. In addition, the reliability of some of the data is questionable, since much of this information is derived from the statements of incoming prisoners and is left unverified. There is no reason to assume that information loss or error is systematically related to ethnicity, which would cast doubt on trends in the data. But rigorous analysis of the interviews of ethnic subgroups (such as young Latin, black or white convicts), may sometimes be impeded by lack of information on other personal characteristics.

Data problems are most acute for the jails surveyed, where personnel sometimes have difficulty locating persons in the system, let alone information about them. Some information loss also occurs in the prisons because most of the men who injure themselves are committed (at least for a short observation period) to the prison mental health facility where file loss or damage is fairly common. Indeed, the problem is so chronic that prison administrators are only mildly surprised when they receive a man from the New York City jails or the prison mental hospital with no background information at all.

The problem of information loss is not as acute for the ethnic samples under consideration as it is for inmates about whom ethnic background is unknown. For the latter group (which we have noted is excluded from this analysis), there is typically no correctional data at all. On the other hand, there is some demographic and criminal history information on virtually all men for whom ethnicity is known. The validity of background information on the ethnic samples nevertheless remains undetermined. Thus while background variables are

Table A-9
Breakdown of Demographic Variables

Category	Code	Classification(s) for Analysis
1. Age	Verbatim (years)	Adolescent (under 21) Adult (over 21)
2. Marital status	1. Single 2. Married (legally) 3. Married (common law) 4. Separated, widowed, divorced	Married/all other categories
3. Place of birth	Region: 1. Northeastern U.S. 2. Southeastern U.S. 3. Other U.S. 4. Foreign born	1. Northeastern U.S./ all other categories 2. Southeastern U.S./ all other categories 3. Other U.S./all other categories 4. Foreign born/all other categories
4. Residence on arrest	A. Population size of residence: 1. 500,000 or more (e.g., New York City) 2. 100,000 to 499,999 (e.g., Buffalo) 3. 50,000 to 99,999 (e.g., Utica) 4. 30,000 to 49,999 (e.g., Auburn) 5. 10,000 to 29,999 (e.g., Amsterdam) 6. Less than 9,999 (e.g., Sprakers) B. Area Of Residence In New York State	A-1. Urban area (50,000+ or more/nonurban area) A-2. Major urban area 500,000 or more/rural area (less than 10,000) B-1. Upstate/downstate[a]

Table A-9—Continued

Category	Code	Classification(s) for Analysis
5. Narcotic drug addiction	Present/absent	Present/absent
6. Alcohol dependence	1. None 2. Mild 3. Moderate 4. Severe	Present (severe)/absent (all others)
7. Occupational status	1. Unemployed 2. Unskilled or low-skilled labor (e.g., carpenter's helper) 3. Unskilled or low-skilled service work (porter, counter man) 4. Skilled labor (crafts, e.g., mason) 5. Skilled service work (semiwhite-collar jobs, such as sales)	1. Unemployed, unskilled, or low-skilled jobs (labor and service) High-skilled jobs (labor and service) 2. Unemployed/skilled service work
8. Occupational stability	Length of employment prior to confinement	Stable (3 months of continuous work at stated profession)/unstable (less than 3 months of work at stated profession)
9. Educational achievement	1. Grade school attendance 2. High school attendance 3. High school graduation 4. Education beyond high school	1. Grade school attendance/all other categories 2. Grade school or high school attendance/all other categories

[a]Downstate New York was defined as New York City, Long Island, and all areas included within a 50-mile radius of midtown Manhattan.

Table A-10
Breakdown of Indices of Criminal Conduct and Confinement Experience

Category	Code	Classification(s) for Analysis
1. Arrest history	Verbatim (number of arrests)	Present/absent
2. Prior sentenced jail terms served	Verbatim (number of sentences served)	Present/absent
3. Prior prison terms served	Verbatim (number of sentences served)	Present/absent
4. Current offense	1. Violent (murder, manslaughter, assault, kidnapping, rape)	Present/absent
	2. Property crimes – major (robbery, burglary, grand larceny)	Present/absent
	3. Property Crimes – minor (petit larceny, criminal mischief, trespass, possession of stolen property)	Present/absent
	4. Addiction-related (possession, sale, or use of drugs; crimes related to excessive alcohol consumption)	Present/absent
	5. Sexual deviance (sodomy, sexual abuse, exhibitionism)	Present/absent
	6. Impulsive or "one-shot" offenses (arson, reckless endangerment, criminally negligent homicide, forgery, bad checks)	Present/absent

Table A-10—Continued

Category	Code	Classification(s) for Analysis
5. Offense history	Violent crime(s)	Present/absent
	Property crime(s)	Present/absent
	Drug crime(s)	Present/absent
6. Maximum sentence	Verbatim (years)	Short (less than 10 years)
		Long (over 10 years)
7. Self-injury incidents in confinement	Verbatim (number of incidents)	1. Present/absent
		2. One/multiple
8. Penal setting of self-injury	Specific facility (where possible) or prison/jail	Prison/jail

[a]Downstate New York was defined as New York City, Long Island, and all areas included within a 50-mile radius of midtown Manhattan.

controlled for in the analysis of ethnic crisis patterns (see Chapter 4), some statistical trends (or the absence of same) may be misleading. Interview material is therefore used to ensure that statistical findings are plausibly related to the concerns of crisis-prone men, and to identify and explore relationships that may be masked by missing or unreliable background data (see Chapters 5-7).

Note

1. J. Gibbs Doctoral Prospectus, School of Criminal Justice, State University of New York at Albany, 1974).

Appendix B

An Autopsy of Stress

The following is an excerpted crisis interview. The account is purposely brief and serves only to expose the reader to an example of the interview schedule as it was deployed with men in crisis.

Johnson:
Maybe you can give me some idea of what the problem was?

CX 49:
It was a long time ago, about 10 months ago. At the time—you are aware that prisons have homosexuality here—I'll put it this way, my mate went home. I call it her and I almost fell in love with her, I could say. That's how much the relationship meant to me. I sort of lost my head because he went home and I felt sorry for myself, like I lost him. And I felt hurt inside. To me it was one of the worst feelings in the world. See I've never had anybody. And when you meet somebody and you really get to know these people you want to stay with them. I broke up. I just hung up because of it. And I still haven't quite gotten over it. What I did I regret, but I know why I done it.

Johnson:
I guess you must have known for a while that—should I say he or she?

CX 49:
She.

Johnson:
—when she was leaving. Did she get parole?

CX 49:
No, she went back to court. She got sent loose.

Johnson:
Did you know this was coming up?

CX 49:
No I didn't.

Johnson:
Oh, so this was quite a shock.

CX 49:
Yeah.

161

Johnson:

Did you get to see her again after that court appearance or did she leave right from there?

CX 49:

She left right from there. I did get to see her though when I was on the streets. I was out on parole.

Johnson:

Were you getting along then?

CX 49:

Yeah.

Johnson:

But at that time it was sort of like she was here one day and gone the next. Did you mourn for a while over this or did you just do it right away? I realize it was a painful period for you. Did this hit you right away or did you live with it for a while?

CX 49:

I got pissed off right away. And I still got the same attitude. As you probably noticed my attitude when you walked in here. The sinister attitude I had since then.

Johnson:

How long did you carry this attitude and feeling before you hurt yourself? A couple of days, a couple of weeks?

CX 49:

It was about three hours.

Johnson:

So it really got down on you?

CX 49:

Yeah.

Johnson:

Looking back on this do you think you could describe some of the thoughts and feelings you had when you hurt yourself? Do you remember some of these feelings?

CX 49:

Yeah, definitely. The feeling that she didn't want me no more. I was thinking about that. A feeling that she rejected me, by leaving me, and just an out and out feeling that everyone was against me. Because she had left, I actually believed that the institution was taking her away from me. This is what I believed.

163

Johnson:

So you not only had the feeling that you personally were being cut loose, but that these people here were responsible for it?

CX 49:

Yeah . . . Well, I was very paranoid at the time she did leave. Not only was I pissed off, but I was afraid. Which is really what paranoia is, being afraid.

Johnson:

Afraid to be alone in this case?

CX 49:

Yes. To be alone in this case. I was that much paranoid.

Johnson:

Were you sort of afraid that you couldn't create another relationship as satisfying as that? Like this would end the best thing.

CX 49:

Yeah, that's exactly it. To give you the truth, she was just as good as a real woman. . . .

Johnson:

You say you hurt yourself within three hours of getting this news, could you give me some idea of how this occurred?

CX 49:

I'll explain it to you as it happened. I think that would be the best way. The first thing that happened, Paula told me that she was going to court. It was the same day that she was there. We were together at the time and she told me that she may come back and she may not, she wasn't sure. So we spent some time to ourselves, we went away by ourselves. We said our goodbyes. And she left at one o'clock and went back to Rochester. About a week later I received a letter from her stating that she had been released and that she would write to me and send me packages and stuff. When I read the letter I felt a change of emotion in me. 'Cause here I had been waiting for a week. Now you must understand this when a person waits for someone that he loves, it's a feeling that they're away and you're lonely. And when you think that they are about to return you get happier and happier as the day comes for their return. And then you rejoice when you see them. Well, what happened when I received the letter was from rejoicing to at least hearing from her, when I saw the name, I said wow, at least she cared enough to write me. But then when I read the letter it changed from a feeling of rejoicing to a feeling of remorse, not really hate, but of loneliness and of losing my reliance in myself. Saying to myself that I wasn't man enough for her and a feeling that it was the end.

Johnson:

So you took this on yourself that it was your responsibility that she was gone?

CX 49:

Yes.

Johnson:

When you say the ball game is over, do you mean that you began to consider taking your life?

CX 49:

Yes, that did run through my mind at the time. I did believe very sincerely that without her life was no good. But then again I had to rationalize and perceive the thought of what would happen if I did cut up and it would be my life and I would never see her again. These thoughts ran through my mind also. So the other was stronger than the foremost thoughts.

Johnson:

How long after you got there did you hurt yourself? Was it after you got the letter?

CX 49:

It was after the letter, about two hours later.

Johnson:

Do you think you could give me a picture of those two hours.

CX 49:

Well, to anyone that was outside and saw the condition I was in, it would have been two hours of hell. I went from pacing the floor of my cell and I was very disgusted. Even if anyone walked by my gate, get the fuck away from my gate. Get the fuck out of my gate. I was really upset because of this. Even one of my closest friends here couldn't talk to me because I wouldn't talk to him and I didn't want to talk to anyone. I wanted to think this out for myself. This is the feeling that I had. Now if you can imagine the traits of being angry and concerned, in other words worried, but being angry at the same time. Also a feeling of unself-reliance and a feeling of pity for yourself, all rolled into one, you could pretty much get a good picture of what I was like at that time.

Johnson:

So you were angry at the situation and at the same time you were feeling responsible and sorry for yourself and sort of incompetent all rolled into one. Now, how did you translate that into hurting yourself? Was that "let me end this because there's nothing to live for?" Or was that "let me communicate something to someone?"

CX 49:

What I decided was that I was hurt and it was time that I talk to somebody. But since I had never had any relationships with any of the staff here I thought it was about time that something happened. So I decided that the best way to do it was put on a show. In other words, to do a bug out. Not really bugging out, but just making believe that you were and wanting to talk to somebody. That you knew he was there to listen.

Johnson:

Did you think that these people were particularly able to help you?

CX49:

No I didn't, because at the time I didn't know any of them. I had no relationship with them and I thought it was about time that I got a relationship with somebody because I was pretty messed up.

Johnson:

Was it your assumption that ultimately they could do something or do a better job for you than a friend could?

CX 49:

Yes, Back in those days, the people that I hung around with were my cousin that was here and Charlie, my blood brother. And they were the same type of people that I was. So naturally it's not going to give me any help to go to them.

Johnson:

When you wanted to get help, was it help for these feelings that you had of incompetence or was it getting yourself in some kind of relationship or was it for some other reason? What did you want to get help for?

CX 49:

I wanted to get help in how to overcome this. How to overcome the feelings that I had at the time. I didn't know quite clearly how to handle myself.

Johnson:

Was that a little unnerving for you?

CX 49:

Yes it was. As a matter of fact they had me on some kind of medicine for a period of time.

Johnson:

In other words, these two hours of hell were not only painful in the sense that you agonized over these issues, but also you were wondering what the hell was going on?

CX 49:

Yeah.

Johnson:

When you came to hurt yourself was it as clear as saying "I know I need help and I'm going to get it by doing this" or was it a thing that was getting out of control and you sort of knew in the back of your mind that this would bring some sort of help and at the time you were sort of trapped in the middle?

CX 49:

Yes. That's exactly it.

Johnson:

Would that be sort of an unclear thinking period?

CX 49:

I must contradict that one point. When I eventually got around to doing what I was going to do my conscious sort of denied that I would get any help and my subconscious sort of knew that it was going to happen.

Johnson:

What was your conscious self doing?

CX 49:

My conscious self was completely screwed up. . . .

Johnson:

Is this something that you were aware of at that time when it was happening?

CX 49:

Right now this is a very good feeling to me because I'm looking back on it. Nowadays I can look at it from a different viewpoint than I did a few months ago. Right now I am virtually hashing it out in my mind and it's a good feeling.

Johnson:

Is it the sort of feeling that you understand something that was at one time taboo?

CX 49:

Yes. It was like a mystery at the time it happened.

Johnson:

Do you think at any point, let's say as this thing, this idea and feeling was becoming bigger and harder to handle, did you see any options at that time besides hurting yourself? Did you see other things you could have done?

CX 49:

Yes. I actually felt that if I did cut up somehow Paula would get word of it and come back to me.

Johnson:

So it had a number of messages then?

CX 49:

Yes, I also had the feeling that if I cut up the institution would bring her back. . . .

Johnson:

When you look back on that do you see this as a product of all this stress? Or did you see it as a fantasy that you needed to get through that period?

CX 49:

I seen it as a stress and strain to my mind. I didn't take it as just my relationship with Paula, but with my relationship with human beings themselves on the outside of these walls and also within it.

Johnson:

She had come to represent as many things as you ever had?

CX 49:

That's right.

Johnson:

This situation was tragic to you in a very full sense. . . . As this was coming up you were getting more upset and this idea of cutting up is becoming bigger and you think that by cutting up it might actually undo the situation that has caused all this pain. It might be a solution. Did any other solutions occur to you or did this seem like the only way to do what you thought had to be done?

CX 49:

There was no solution at that time that I could think of except that . . . this seemed like the right thing to do at that time.

Johnson:

Once this idea popped into your mind and stuck did you have any feelings like maybe I shouldn't do this or may I should give it some more thought?

CX 49:

No. I had no feelings of remorse. Actually I didn't give a damn. . . . I felt at that time that without her love life was just no good.

Appendix C

Typology of Breakdowns

I. Themes related to coping (man and prison)
  A. Helplessness and resentment
    1. *Sanctuary search:* An effort to escape from redundant preoccupations, particularly with regard to problems in the outside world or in the person's own situation—to which he finds no solution or closure; the object is to break the unproductive cycle, and to secure peace of mind.
    2. *Self-victimization:* A statement of one's inability to endure the self-defined status of victim of continued arbitrariness, inequity, or abuse by the criminal justice system or its personnel. The person gives notice of his helplessness (demanding a truce) or advertises accumulated resentment (where extrapunitive reactions are deemed unsafe).
  B. Social isolation
    1. *Isolation panic:* A demand for release from panic-producing isolation, where the person finds his confinement oppressive and fear inspiring, intolerable, and obsessive; where he dwells on the duration and/or circumstances of his confinement, on his own discomfort, on his inability to engage in prison activities and social life.
  C. Need for staff assistance in selective coping
    1. *Self-classification:* An effort to communicate to staff the importance and seriousness of one's need for a specific milieu among those available in prison. The inmate here differentiates—within the prison—social or physical environments in which he can operate, and setting he finds it impossible to adjust to. He underlines the seriousness and importance of the distinction.
    2. *Aid seeking:* A demand for staff services that cannot be ignored, as the inmate sees it. It occurs where a physical problem becomes the focus of the person's discontent, and where he becomes obsessed with the need for attention to his complaint, and upset about staff failure to comply or respond to direct requests.
II. Themes related to negative self-assessment (self and others)
  A. Career and self-worth (hopelessness and self-doubt)
    1. *Self-deactivation:* An expression of disinterest in continued day-to-day life, which is seen as an extrapolation or continuation of past failures. This conclusion follows an inventory in which the person becomes increasingly more apathetic and discouraged—where he sees no future role for himself, and loses interest and drive.

169

2. *Self-sentencing:* An effort to cut losses and to provide relief to others. Follows an inventory of past (and current) conduct vis-a-vis friends and relatives, which sparks shame, guilt, self-condemnation, and poor prognosis for a constructive future. At this stage, the person adjudges himself useless—as a complete liability to himself and other people.

3. *Self-retaliation:* Self-retaliation or self-punishment, where the person feels he is placed in an intolerable position as a result of his own past acts, and feels angry and resentful at himself.

B. Resourcelessness and fear

1. *Fate avoidance:* A conclusion relating to one's inability to survive current or impending social situations (usually involving other inmates) that one fears because one sees oneself as weak, ineffective, or unable to respond.

C. Need for significant others

1. *Self-linking:* A protest against intolerable separation from significant others, against perceived abandonment by them, or against the inability to function as constructive group member. A rejection of the possibility of an independent life, where termination of constructive contact is experienced. The person here feels his well-being tied to his relationship (usually, with his family) and sees no satisfactory existence without such contact or link.

2. *Self-certification:* An effort to convince the other party in a degenerating or terminating relationship of one's seriousness, affect, or inability to survive. A dramatic demonstration of resentment self-pity, or personal sincerity.

III. Themes Related to impulse-management

A. Capitulation to internal pressure (catharsis and self-hate)

1. *Self-alienation:* A reluctant or passive compliance with alien but powerful impulses and commands that direct the person to destroy himself.

2. *Self-release:* A catharsis or strategic loss of control designed to discharge aggressive feelings and to end tension and discomfort related to such feelings. Occurs as a temporary loss of contact with reality after a cumulation of resentment, tension, and anger, and is followed by emotional drain and experienced relief.

B. Projected or subjective danger

1. *Self-escape:* An effort to preserve sanity—or to escape—where the person experiences destructive impulses that are strong and unpleasantly tension provoking. The person may feel disturbed by imagined threats combined with experiences of his own destructive potential.

2. *Self-preservation:* An attempt to escape cumulating harm where the person builds up the conviction that he is in substantial physical danger from pervasive and all-powerful enemies. The inmate may destroy himself—as he sees it—one step ahead of feared destruction by others.

C. Need for assistance with internal control

1. *Self-intervention:* A demand for professional (mental health) help with the understanding and control of one's own impulses and moods; a last-ditch effort to secure such help through action where verbal requests are seen as nonproductive.

Index

Index

Abandonment, crisis of, 85–88, 125
Adaptation, of black inmates, 112. *See also* Black inmates
Addicts, Latin, 87. *See also* Drug addicts; Heroin addicts
Adjustment, of adolescents, 137; of "average" male, 1; cultural differences in, xvi, 13; modes of, 5; promotion of, 135. *See also* Coping
Adolescence, 8; and prison risk, 45
Adolescents, adjustment problems of, 137; fate avoidance crises among, 68, 70; in prison, 123; self-certification crises among, 72–73
Age, self-injury and, 43
Aggression, expression of, 99
Aid seeking, 169
Anxiety, 81–85. *See also* Crises
Appalachian whites, 21. *See also* White inmates
Arrests, and prison risk, 47; self-injury and, 43
Authority, of Latin inmates, 94; of prison system, 90

Bettelheim, Bruno, 8
Black inmates, xv; ameliorating stress of, 137; breakdowns among, 57–60, 104; crisis intervention for, 136–137; crisis prone, 76, 77, 80; cultural responses of, 23; education of, 49; fate avoidance crises of, 56; folklore heroes of, 19; isolation panic among, 63; prison behavior of, 135; prison problems of, 74–76; and prison stress, 8; relative prevalence of, 144; self-destructive behavior of, 18; self-preservation crises among, 66–67; socialization of, 16
Breakdowns, 31, 126; attitudes toward, 7; among black inmates, 57–60,

104; cultural context of, 10; of Latin inmates, 55-57, 95; typology of, 35, 36, 169–171; of white inmates, 60–71, 77

Censoriousness, 19
Chicanos, education of, 49; group support of, 16. *See also* Latin inmates
Chi Square Test, 54
Cobbs, P., 17
Comparison sample, 147–152
Concentration camps, Nazi, 8
Conflicts, homosexual, 2 (*see also* Homosexuality); sibling, 93–94
Confrontations, dead-end, 107–107; peer, 106, 129
Cool, 19, 100; appearance of, 7; of black prisoners, 112
Coping, 13; attitudes toward, 102; failure of, 30 (*see also* Crises); with family support loss, 84, 89–95; patterns of, 21–22; strategies of, 8, 38, 104, 122
Correctional managers, 138. *See also* Prison staff
Crimes, addiction related, 48. *See also* Drug addicts; Offense
Criminal justice system, attitudes toward, 99, 118
Crises, of abandonment, 85–88, 125; fate avoidance, 61–62, 68, 70, 93, 116, 170; impulse management, 54, 74; index of, 30; response to, 52; self-assessment, 77, 138; self-certification, 72–73, 123; self-escape, 108; self-intervention, 71; self-linking, 58, 59, 60, 85, 101, 102, 170; self-preservation, 60; self-retaliation, 119, 120; types of, 35. *See also* Breakdowns
Crisis intervention, 136
Cultural group, 1. *See also* Ethnicity
Culture, and stress, 136

175

About the Author

Robert Johnson received his undergraduate training in psychology at Fairfield University and received the Ph.D. in criminal justice from the State University of New York at Albany. He has been an Honorable Woodrow Wilson Fellow and a Herbert H. Lehman Fellow. Dr. Johnson is currently Assistant Professor of Criminal Justice at the University of North Carolina at Charlotte.